IMAGES
of America

LAS VEGAS

IMAGES
of America

LAS VEGAS

Mitch Barker

ARCADIA
PUBLISHING

Published by Arcadia Publishing
Charleston, South Carolina

Library of Congress Control Number: 2013948884

For all general information, please contact Arcadia Publishing:
Telephone 843-853-2070
Fax 843-853-0044
E-mail sales@arcadiapublishing.com
For customer service and orders:
Toll-Free 1-888-313-2665

Visit us on the Internet at www.arcadiapublishing.com

To those who went before us and those who will come after

CONTENTS

ACKNOWLEDGMENTS

The author is grateful for help from the Las Vegas Citizens Committee for Historic Preservation (CCHP), the staff at New Mexico Highlands University's Donnelly Library, and the City of Las Vegas Museum and Rough Rider Memorial Collection (RR) in procuring information and graphics for this book. Thanks to Jeannie McKinley and Martha McCaffrey at CCHP. The images in this book are courtesy of:

AL	Annabelle Lucero Collection
BD	Bob Dalton Collection
CLLV	Carnegie Library, Las Vegas
CT	Connie Trujillo
DL	Donnelly Library
DA	Donnelly Library, Arrott Collection
EB	Elmo Baca Collection
FB	Father Burke Collection
FD	Mrs. F.D. Rieniet Collection
FL	Fred Lewis
ILV	Illustrated Las Vegas 1903
JC	Josie Crespin
JH	Josephine Hayes Collection
LB	Les Botorr Collection
LF	Lee Fidel Collection
LP	Lynn Perrigo Collection
LVO	Las Vegas *Optic*
OLOS	Our Lady of Sorows
OLOS JD	Our Lady of Sorows, Jacob Duran Collection
OLOS MS	Our Lady of Sorows, Margaret Sanchez Collection
OLOS MT	Our Lady of Sorows, Mrs. Torres Collection
OLOS PC	Our Lady of Sorows, Pita Ciddio Collection
PSLV	Photographic Survey of Las Vegas
RH	Rose Hanosh
RL	Rudy Lovato Collection
SM	San Miguel County Abstract Company
ST	Sandra Trujillo Collection
TG	Tony Gallegos
TS	Tony Sanchez Collection

INTRODUCTION

The Las Vegas area has long been a place for gathering. Geography is the reason. The townsite, its meadows, and its surroundings lie on a natural pathway through the mountains, providing an easy crossing of the Gallinas River, where people and vehicles could avoid struggling down and back up the many nearby canyons. Thus, nature selected its place on a path taken time and again by those afoot and in wagons, later by surveyors for the railroad, and finally, highway engineers.

Within a few miles of Las Vegas are remains of homes and the art of people who lived from 900 to 1,100 years ago. In their villages were Plains pottery mixed with that of the Rio Grande Puebloan people to the west. The mixing of Plains and Pueblo Indian artifacts provides evidence that from earliest days it was a meeting place.

In 1540, Hernando de Alvarado, a scout for Francisco Vázquez de Coronado, heard a tale of villages of gold to the east. The Indians shared this in hopes that the visitors would lose themselves on the plains. Alvarado and Coronado determined to find the treasures. Thus, early Spanish visitors passed through the Las Vegas area and on to disappointment in Kansas. Thwarted in finding gold but not entirely discouraged, the Spanish stayed to became masters of the Southwest.

Much later, near where Las Vegas would arise, another meeting marked the end of Spanish rule. Trade along the Santa Fe Trail from the United States, forbidden by the government, took place anyway. New Mexico needed goods. Spain was far away, and the Americans were much closer. Where there is a desire for goods, commerce finds a way.

In 1821, just south of the site of Las Vegas, 400 soldiers, militia, and some Pueblo Indians met a train of Missouri traders headed by William Becknell. They told the Missourians that Mexico had thrown off Spanish rule. Commerce with the United States on the Santa Fe Trail was now open.

In the early part of the 19th century, there was no settlement where Las Vegas now stands, but it was a prominent point on the trail, according to historian Ralph Emerson Twitchell. Travelers could cross the Rio Gallinas there without difficulty. El Creston, called that for resembling the fin on a conquistador's helmet, marked the first significant hill on the trail west of the crossing and the last leg of the journey into Santa Fe.

Settlers would only trickle in for fear of raids by Utes, Apaches, and Comanches. In 1832, a traveler from the United States found only "a little hovel at the foot of a cliff." However, by 1845, there were a hundred houses where Las Vegas is now.

The next major area event came 25 years after the opening of trade with the United States. The citizens of Las Vegas were alarmed to learn their country was at war with the United States. Yankee soldiers were moving to take their land. As Mexico's easternmost settlement, Las Vegas would be first to experience invasion.

Their biggest dread involved religion; they were fearful that the Protestant United States would not allow Catholic New Mexicans to practice their faith. As the invaders approached, women and children fled onto El Creston behind the town. When Stephen W. Kearny, commander of the Americans, arrived, he proclaimed them absolved of their Mexican citizenship and pointedly announced they were free to practice their faith. As long as they were law abiding, no harm would come to them.

Another meeting took place; this time, Coronado's children met with Northern Europeans. They would build a town together. The future would sometimes be difficult. Violence and misunderstanding were to come, but the two also demonstrated admirable cooperation.

When the railroad arrived from the northeast, the town became a violent place as prominent outlaws of the era drifted in. There were clashes, sometimes daily, between order and lawlessness until the anarchic element moved on or died and civil peace was obtained.

Las Vegas appeared likely to become the major city of the territory, with a greater population than Albuquerque or Santa Fe. It served a trading area greater than both. In time, however, the promise dimmed, and Las Vegas contented itself with a diminished but rewarding destiny.

About 100 years after Kearny's speech, Las Vegas was building motor courts for tourists. In those early days of automobile travel, there were few cars, but hardy travelers crossing New Mexico came within five miles of Las Vegas on Route 66 and frequently stopped for fuel, food, or rest. What John Steinbeck would later call "America's Mother Road" entered from Texas at Tucumcari, headed west to Santa Rosa, north to Romeroville—at the outskirts of Las Vegas—and through Glorieta Pass to Santa Fe, then south to Albuquerque. The highway brought travelers to the Las Vegas area until 1937, when the alignment was changed.

Tuberculosis sufferers also gathered in the Las Vegas area. Until the development of penicillin, there was no cure for tuberculosis but dry air and rest, with the former abundant in the climate here. Patients endured outdoor life in all weather, bundled in blankets and sheltered from precipitation, hoping the regimen would heal their damaged lungs.

As word spread about the charm of the nearby resorts in the high country, healthy people came for camping that ranged from rough to luxurious.

Tourism still draws visitors to Las Vegas. Fort Union, two dozen miles north, once was the Army's supply depot for the Southwest. Pecos Pueblo, whose people told Coronado of the golden cities of the plains, is a half-hour drive west. Both are national monuments.

The city itself is an attraction. Unlike Santa Fe, it gets on without a code dictating its adobe homes and businesses. Yet Las Vegas has more buildings in the National Register of Historic Places than the state capital. Las Vegas homes and commercial buildings are a mix of old and young, rich and poor, and thriving and sometimes seedy. It presents an honest face to the world, blemishes and all.

New Mexico Highlands University draws students from throughout the United States. The Armand Hammer United World College of the American West has an even larger expanse of candidates for admission. Students from around the world attend the school and participate in Las Vegas–area cultural and social events in town and at the school.

Meetings and mixing has been the story of this place. We are fortunate that many people left images of their lives behind. This book attempts to bring their stories to life though the photographs that remain.

One

BEFORE 1900

Brig. Gen. Steven Watts Kearny brought the Stars and Stripes to the tiny Mexican village of Las Vegas in August 1846. His biggest problem on arrival was winning the hearts and minds of the people. They thought the Yankee army was bringing rapine and plunder, oppression, robbery of their churches, and desecration of their altars. He settled their fears by telling them that many in his force were Catholics and practiced freely. (DL.)

The first facilities at Montezuma hot springs were very spartan. The American military built this bathhouse at the springs in 1846 for soldiers' relaxation and recreation. This is the earliest known view, dated 1867. The Mexican emperor Montezuma bathed here according to the legend that gave it the name. (LP.)

In 1864, the Las Vegas Hot Springs Company blocked half the springs and pumped the remainder into rooms for treating customers in this hotel. The business advertised cures for rheumatism and skin infections, blood poisoning, gout, glandular diseases, nervous afflictions, mental exhaustion, spinal troubles, ulcers, "female weakness," hay fever, and asthma, among other illness. The photograph is from 1882. (OLOS.)

This 1881 map of Las Vegas land claims shows the original Las Vegas to the west with streets following land contours and the new town with streets in a grid. (SM.)

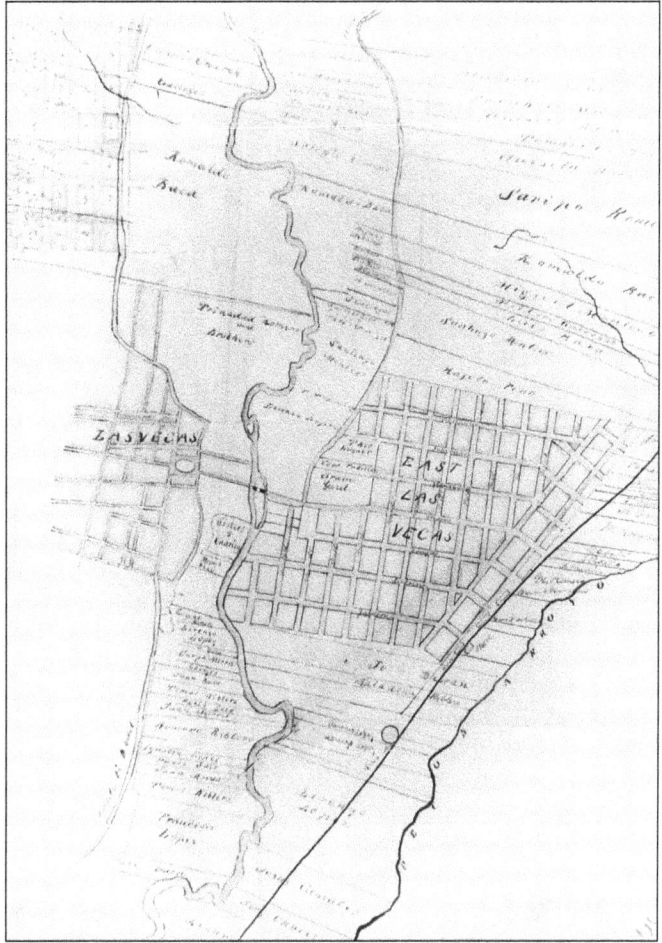

This is the Plaza as it looked in 1879, with the camera trained toward the east. Wagons would arrive from Missouri, coming down the infant Bridge Street in the distance, and take advantage of facilities available in the stores that ringed the empty square before moving on. The route farther west used Pacific Street, which is out of sight beyond the trees on the right. (DL.)

The military was a neighbor to the newly American Las Vegas. To protect the Santa Fe Trail, the Army initially assigned soldiers to a garrison in the town. Later, it established Fort Union, situated about 24 miles away. The fort was the major supply post for Army installations throughout the Southwest and bolstered the Las Vegas economy. These Fort Union officers and their wives pose for this picture in about 1875. (DL.)

In this picture, Fort Union supply wagons await repair and refitting. Spare parts such as wheels are stacked for later use. Notice the saplings carefully supported against the wind that often blows strongly at the fort, which is on an open plain unsheltered by nearby trees or hills. (DL.)

In an example of Fort Union as a self-contained community, troops show off their steam-driven fire engine in the center of this photograph taken about 1875. As Fort Union is about 24 miles from Las Vegas, it could not rely on fire protection arriving from the town and required its own. The fort stored a considerable amount of ammunition and explosives. (DL.)

This is the interior of an officer's quarters at Fort Union. The quarters were duplexes; two families shared one building. The exception was the commanding officer, whose family lived in a single-family home befitting his rank. When a new officer arrived, he and his family would displace those of lower rank. Families moved out of their quarters and down one, displacing the next lower ranking families. (DL.)

The Fort Union hospital was a Mayo Clinic for its day. It had the best care along the Santa Fe Trail and was the place to go if one was ill or injured. Civilians received care at little cost. The hospital was at a distance from the rest of the post to avoid infection and is near today's visitor center. This picture is from about 1875. (DA.)

Fort Union officers' families had to find ways to cope with time that often hung heavy on their hands. Many wives wrote of dealing with the long days and the fort's exposure to days of unrelenting wind. Among other things, they could socialize, hold dances, gossip, and write home. This row of officers' quarters is from 1875. (DA.)

Another group of Fort Union personnel gathered for this picture around 1875. Among the men are some that are not in uniform. Some were employees of the Army, while others were contractors. A general merchant, called a sutler, provided for such personal needs as tobacco, candy, and writing paper. (DA.)

This building held the offices of the *Las Vegas Gazette* at South Pacific and Moreno Streets from 1865 to 1882. In *The Town that Wouldn't Gamble*, Milton Callon writes that the editor of the *Gazette* typified the editorial posture of the time: "They presumed their editorialship vested in them a power to see all things and be able to judge them in their proper perspective. . . . [The editor] took it upon himself to assume the knowledge of the clergy, government officials and the military. . . . He was certain to be right in some categories but the damage done by biased editors was often more lasting than the good." (PSLV.)

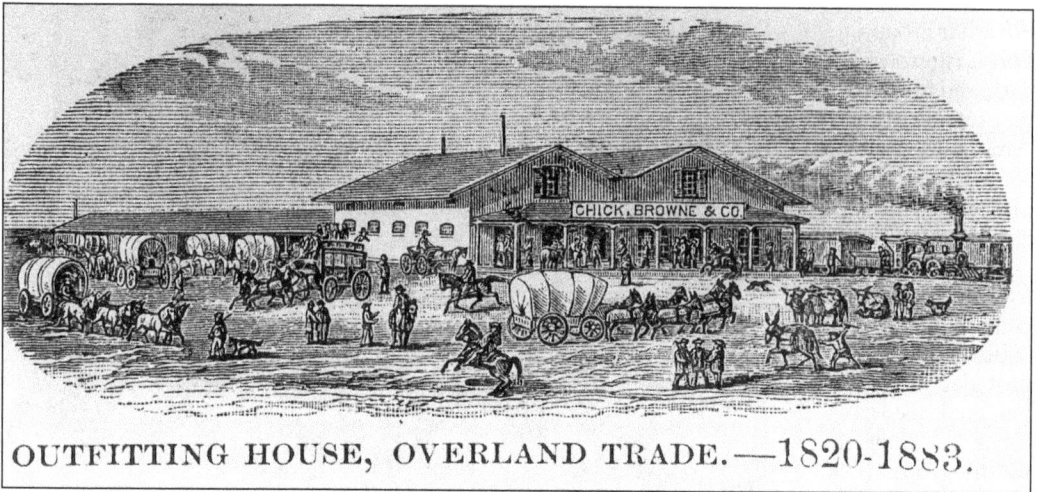

OUTFITTING HOUSE, OVERLAND TRADE.—1820-1883.

This outfitting house for overland trade did business supplying wagons on the Santa Fe Trail from 1820 to 1883 and eventually became Browne and Manzanares Company. (ILV.)

This derrick initially was for a well on the Plaza, but after a short time, it failed to produce water. Thereafter, it conveniently served for hangings. The derrick came down in 1877, about the time this image was captured. Local children dispatching small animals in their backyards after watching public executions was responsible for demands to raze the derrick. However, this may be apocryphal. (FB.)

Seen here are the first graduates of New Mexico Normal University, the class of 1901. Normal school or university was a common term until the 1970s, then the names rapidly dropped out of use. The terms refer to teacher training institutions. The university deemed these five men and eight young ladies ready to take on the education of New Mexico Territory's students for the next generation. Imagine how much they influenced the future. (DL.)

This panorama of early Las Vegas about 1890 is from the ridge east of today's Interstate 25. From left to right, the legible handwritten notations are "Rumaldo Baca's 4 story house" (also know as Baca's Folly, as referenced on page 34), "Court House," "Academy," "Plaza Hotel," "Ilfelds," "Lincoln Park," "Business Dist. R.R. Ave.," "Rosenthal Store & Dance Hall," "Now Pennys," and "La Voz del Pueblo, now Phillips Station & Bus Depot." In the foreground are noted Railroad Avenue and "Now Commerce St." (OLOS.)

The E. Romero Hose and Fire Company owned a fire wagon drawn by horses and 900 feet of hose, which supplied water using a gravity system. If the horses were not available because of illness or some other reason, men had to draw the trucks. Here, in a picture taken about 1890, members ready for a practice run, pulling the truck that is out of sight to the right. (LP.)

At 6,800 feet above sea level, cold days and nights come early and stay late in the Las Vegas area. To keep warm, residents burned the abundant lumber from nearby mountains. Wood vendors like these made a living plying the streets of Las Vegas. These animals and their master pause for a photograph to be taken some time around 1890 on Railroad Avenue. (FD.)

"Mysterious" Dave Mather lived on both sides of the law. At first, he wore a star in Las Vegas and accompanied the sheriff on a raid to enforce an ordinance against wearing guns. The sheriff died in the attempt. Days later, a gang lynched two who killed the sheriff, and Mather helped. Because he took part in the hanging, Mather's time in Las Vegas was over, and he left for Texas. In this photograph, taken about 1890, he might be pondering his direct descent from Cotton Mather, the Puritan theologian. (FB.)

Treated logs initially supported telegraph wires. When the railroad arrived in 1879, logs were milled and coated for use as ties for train tracks. The invention of the telephone and its spread caused even more demand for poles. Hindering the spread of telephone service in some areas was skepticism that the invention would be able to transmit Spanish. In this picture from about 1860, a team pauses to have its picture taken. (FB.)

The first county seat was San Miguel del Bado. It moved to Las Vegas in 1864. The San Miguel County Courthouse, built in 1889, was a Richardsonian Romanesque structure located just east of the present courthouse. The county took down the old courthouse in the 1930s. For construction of the present courthouse, workers removed steps of the old courthouse so building could begin. This picture dates from around 1915. (TS.)

The Montezuma has a long, varied history. The Santa Fe Railroad built the first Montezuma Hotel in 1882. It has been resort, a Mexican Catholic seminary, and a school in real life. In movies, it has been a set several times. On screen, it has been an Adirondack home (*Georgia O'Keeffe*, 1969) and a haunted mansion (*The Evil*, 1978), among many other roles. Here, in one of its early moments, guests relax on the veranda. (FB.)

THE MONTEZUMA AS IT WAS.

This clipping from the Las Vegas *Optic* of January 1884 depicts the first Montezuma Hotel, which was built to attract wealthy patrons. It lasted only a short time before fire destroyed it. The Santa Fe Railroad was not deterred by the loss. It built a second, even grander hotel on the same spot. (DL.)

The PHOENIX

(FORMERLY · MONTESUMA)

Las Vegas Hot Springs

· NEW · MEXICO ·

Within four months of opening, fire ruined much of the second Montezuma hotel. The blaze started in the attic, which firemen could not reach. They were able to get to the two lower stories, so it was not a total loss. After restoration, the Montezuma received a new name referring to its rebirth after the fires. The name did not catch on with the public, and the Santa Fe Railroad resumed using the name of Montezuma. (PSLV.)

The third Montezuma still stands in 2013. The renowned Chicago firm of Birnham and Root designed and constructed the main building on a commanding hill. The company designed many of Chicago's large homes and commercial buildings and pioneered skyscraper design. It famously planned the World's Columbian Exhibition (Chicago World's Fair) in 1893. The third Montezuma opened in 1886 and closed in 1893. It reopened in 1895 and closed again in 1904. (JH.)

The date of this picture is unknown, but it provides an idea of the furnishings in a bedroom at the Montezuma Hotel during its early years. It does not appear elaborate, so this may have been one of the less expensive rooms. The chandelier is for electric light, and there are several chairs for relaxing or chatting between visitors and their guests. (FB.)

A Jewish congregation took root in Las Vegas in 1884. It was the first established in New Mexico Territory. Congregation Montefiore, Reform worshippers, maintained an active group despite a dwindling population until 1931. After that time, a rabbi periodically came from Santa Fe to hold services. The congregation eventually sold the synagogue. Catholics bought the building and moved it to Eighth Street, where it is now the Newman Chapel. (OLOS.)

For some years, a horse- or mule-drawn trolley traveled between the Plaza and the railroad depot. However, a walk was often faster than taking the trolley between the two points. Full fare was a nickel, and the animals averaged 22 miles a day. Feeding time for the animals was 3:00 a.m., 10:30 a.m., 4:30 p.m., and 9:00 p.m. In 1903, the company sold the animals and converted to electricity. This cleaned up the streets. This picture is from about 1870. (OLOS.)

In a noble effort to redirect cravings for that devil alcohol, ladies of the local Women's Christian Temperance Union erected this lion statue in 1896. It was fitted with drinking fountains, and the space around it became known as Lion Park. It was the women's "expectation that an alternate thirst-quencher would reduce saloon patronage." In the background is the Serf Hotel, and on the right is the *Daily Optic* newspaper and print shop. (FB.)

Workmen clamber over Douglas School as it undergoes construction in 1891. The school in new or East Las Vegas was to play a significant role in the education of Las Vegas children for years until the school system razed it in the 1920s. (DL.)

snow scene. Bridge St. cross ... Hot Spgs. Branch. Las Vegas, N. ...

When the Atchison, Topeka & Santa Fe Railroad built the Montezuma Hotel in Gallinas Canyon, it also constructed a spur from Las Vegas to the hot springs and beyond to the ice ponds. Trains carried guests and supplies to the hotel and performed other uses. Someone photographed this train near Bridge Street in about 1890. It might have been en route to load ice from the ponds for use on refrigerated freight cars. (FB.)

This plat of the Montezuma Hotel complex from about 1882 has some elements not greatly different from what still exists, such as the grand hilltop building atop labeled "Montezuma," as well as a park below it and bathhouses at the hot springs across the river. The small lots may have been cottage sites. The plat contains a redundancy, "Rio Gallinas River," indicating that it must have been produced by someone new to the area. (SM.)

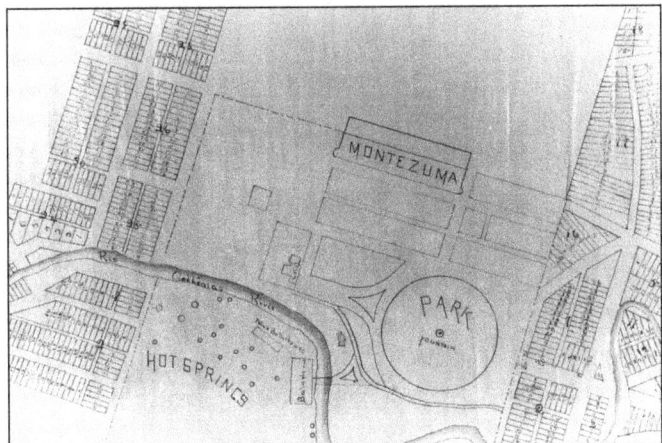

Smells from the Baash Bakery on Bridge Street must have been difficult to pass without stopping to make a purchase. Baash is a Czech or Bohemian surname, so it is likely the proprietor came from what was then the Austro-Hungarian Empire. This picture is from the 1890s, when many people from that part of Europe were coming to America to escape turmoil. (DL.)

This view of Bridge Street in the 1890s looks east. Notice the horse- or mule-drawn trolley tracks in the middle of the street. Also note the wooden sidewalks and awnings over the storefronts. The street is unpaved and would have been a slough following rain or snow with wagons and horses plowing it up. Springer Hall at New Mexico Normal (later Highlands) University is at the top of the hill on the right. (City of Las Vegas Museum and Rough Rider Memorial Collection, 67.42.1.)

Don Trinidad Romero built this expansive home in 1880 about five miles south of Las Vegas. Romero started as a freighter on the Santa Fe Trail. He became New Mexico Territory's delegate to Congress in 1877. The mansion had high-ceilinged rooms paneled in walnut costing $100,000. In it, he entertained Pres. Rutherford B. Hayes and First Lady Lucy Webb Hayes, Pres. Ulysses S. Grant, and Gen. Philip Sherman. Later, the mansion was a tuberculosis sanitarium and dude ranch. In 1932, it was destroyed by fire. (DL.)

This horse-drawn trolley stops at the southwest corner of the Plaza in about 1890. The buildings in the background are also of interest. On the left is the Rosenwald building, which housed the First National Bank. That institution gave birth to the First National Bank in Albuquerque and the First National Bank in El Paso. The building now holds the West Las Vegas Schools administrative offices. (DL.)

The Las Vegas Academy opened in 1880. The town's Protestant churches operated this academy, which was located on the corner of Twelfth and Lincoln Streets. It is likely that the town's Protestants felt rather besieged in an area where the overwhelming majority of residents were faithful adherents of the Catholic Church. (FB.)

A group of 12 Las Vegas College students and their teacher posed for this studio picture in 1881. As mentioned above, the Catholic Church has the majority of adherents in the Las Vegas area. In September 1884, a Jesuit father assumed duties as the town's first pastor. (OLOS.)

Robert Taupert established a jewelry store in a booming Las Vegas. He advertised, "One price to all and that in plain figures. One quality and that the best for the price." The building at 606–608 Douglas Avenue was probably made of bricks shipped from Trinidad, Colorado, as those locally produced were soft. This picture of the Taupert shop is from about 1890. (CT.)

BUFFALO HALL.

The Finest and Cosiest Resort For Gentlemen in the City.

Billiards,   Pool Table
Ten Pin Alley. Shooting Gallery.

Fresh Keg Beer Always on Tap at Five Cents a Schooner.

Citizens and Strangers are Respectfully Invited to Call.

BRIDGE STREET, WEST LAS VEGAS, NEXT TO THE GAZETTE OFFICE.

LAS VEGAS BREWERY
AND
Bottling Association,
Las Vegas, New Mexico.

Our beer is brewed from the choicest malt and hops and warranted to give entire satisfaction. Our bottled beer is equal to any in the country. Orders respectfully solicited.
Telephone No. 33.⅔   G. A. ROTHGEB, Prop'r.

Las Vegas citizens and visitors enjoyed beer, as these newspaper ads from about 1890 attest. Buffalo Hall had been in business many years by that time and provided a variety of diversions as well as liquid refreshment. (DL.)

29

The Douglas school was the first in New Mexico built with public tax funds. This photograph is from 1897. The building was near Douglas Avenue and Eighth Street. The school system remodeled the structure in the year this image was captured, but it was damaged by fire in 1926. The school system then razed it. (DL.)

"We'll tell Dewey that we saw you" and "We remember the Maine" are on the side of these railcars flanked by Las Vegas–area residents who are sending their young neighbors off to Cuba in 1898 to fight in the Spanish-American War. Commodore George Dewey easily defeated a Spanish naval squadron in Manila Bay early in the war. The USS Maine exploded and sank in Havana Harbor, killing 266 sailors. Many Americans blamed the Maine explosion on Spain, and it led to the war. (City of Las Vegas Museum and Rough Rider Memorial Collection, 2010.13.1.)

This father and child were looking for a handout on Railroad Avenue, probably in the late 1800s. There was no social safety net in those days—no Social Security System, no unemployment benefits, and no government aid finding work for the unemployed. Even for those lucky enough to have jobs, the workweek was usually seven days long. (FD.)

In this portrait is the hermit of Hermit Peak as a young man. He was born in Italy and attended seminary but left over theological differences. He traveled through many countries, mostly by foot, before arriving in Las Vegas. He lived in a cave near Romeroville at first and then on what people at the time called Tecolote Peak, which is now named for him. After leaving this area, he went to Las Cruces, where Native Americans evidently killed him. (OLOS.)

This mansion once stood across from Our Lady of Sorrows church. Margarito Romero, who also owned El Porvenir Resort and the Las Vegas Railway and Power Company, was the proud possessor of the mansion. His power company both ran the trolley and provided the town with electricity. (Dr. W.P. Mills, courtesy City of Las Vegas Museum and Rough Rider Memorial Collection, 67.9.46.)

The Las Vegas Military Band in this 1890s photograph had a more martial appearance than the one on this book's cover. The band changed its appearance several times over the years, as evidenced through these pages. No doubt there were times when donors helped with uniform costs, as well as times when the members themselves had to dig in their pockets to outfit the band. (City of Las Vegas Museum and Rough Rider Memorial Collection, 72.17.1.)

This is the interior of the Bank Saloon on Bridge Street. There are spittoons on the floor for tobacco-chewing patrons. Otherwise, it only partly conforms to the Hollywood version of a saloon. The mirror is rather small, not nearly large enough for spectacularly shattering in gunfights. While there are pictures of women on the wall, they are tastefully clothed. One customer lifts a toast toward the camera. (LP.)

Don Jose Albino Baca built this three-story mansion in old or west Las Vegas between 1850 and 1855. He owned thousands of sheep, hundreds of cattle and oxen, and considerable land. This 1930s photograph is from the Historic American Buildings Survey. (DL.)

Rumauldo Baca, believing that the railroad coming down from Colorado would build its tracks into the existing, or old, Las Vegas, had this structure built to contain storerooms on the first level with offices and meeting rooms on the upper stories. However, when the Santa Fe Railroad laid its tracks some distance east, the building was not convenient to arriving and departing trains. Rather cruelly, people started calling it "Baca's Folly." Across the street is Our Lady of Sorrows Church. (FB.)

The Plaza, pictured here in 1889, appears to have been a pleasant place to spend some time. There were well-established trees for shade and paths for strolling. A picket fence around the perimeter may have helped keep loose animals out of the park. By 1903, the fence was gone. The sign is illegible here but may read "Keep off the Grass." (FB.)

34

The Santa Fe Railroad built this bridge over Agua Zarca Arroyo southwest of Las Vegas. After the railroad put in shoring along the right and left banks of the arroyo, a much smaller bridge replaced this one. The replacement bridge is still in use and is visible from Interstate 25. This picture is from 1892. (FB.)

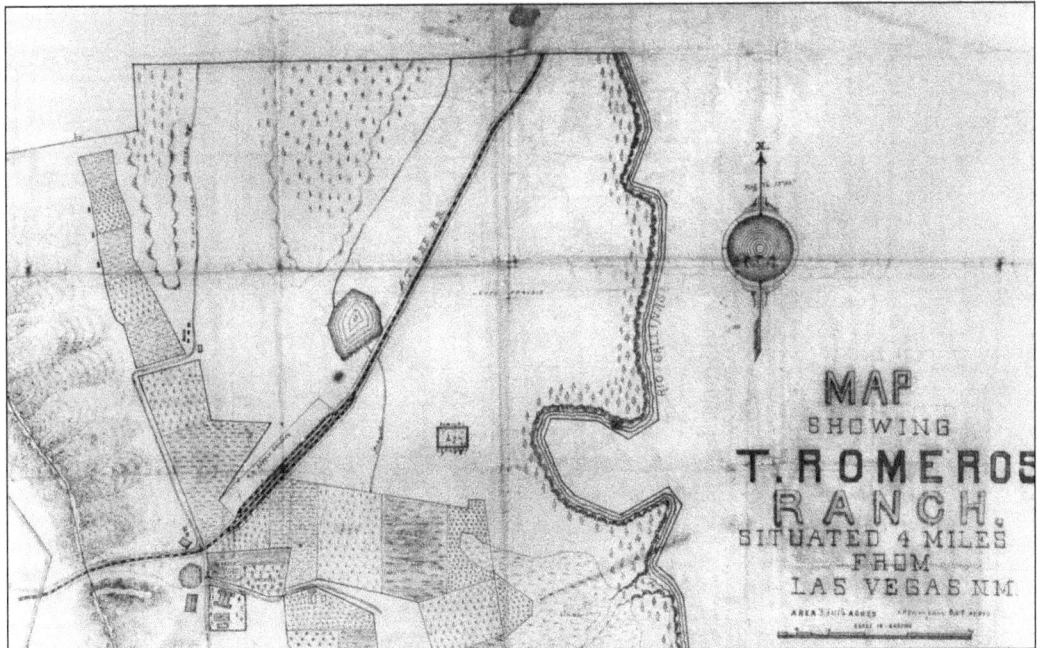

Trinidad Romero's ranch, situated just north of Romeroville about five miles south of Las Vegas, is the main feature of this map. Of particular interest is in the lower left corner, where the Santa Fe Railroad (today's Burlington Northern Santa Fe) tracks ran. It is also where, in later years, highway engineers blasted a cut through El Creston for Interstate 25. The road cut provides a revealing look at sedimentary layers that were tilted sharply as the southern Rockies arose. (SM.)

America's western frontier was very dependent on its newspapers. Las Vegas was no different. The forbears, with fewer sources of information and entertainment that are available today, depended greatly on print. Usually, there were at least two Las Vegas newspapers but often more, in English and Spanish. This is the office of *El Independiente*. It was popular, influential, and Republican. (FB.)

On June 24, 1899, a crowd of 5,000 waited for Theodore Roosevelt, then governor of New York, to arrive at Las Vegas by train. The occasion was the first Rough Rider reunion following the Spanish-American War. Roosevelt had recruited most of his Rough Riders from northeast New Mexico, southern Colorado, west Texas, and Oklahoma. The Rough Riders selected Las Vegas to host their gathering because New Mexico had supplied the greater portion of Roosevelt's men. (JC.)

Theodore "Teddy" Roosevelt addresses attendees from the stands while wearing his campaign hat at the first Rough Rider reunion in Las Vegas. Roosevelt chose the reunion to let the nation know for the first time that he would be available to serve as president. (City of Las Vegas Museum and Rough Rider Memorial Collection, 2010.13.1.)

While Roosevelt had a room at the Hotel Castañeda, he also joined his men for overnights in their tents in Lincoln Park. Here, he visits with an unidentified comrade, an officer who carries a saber and is no doubt a fellow veteran of the campaign in Cuba. He is possibly Leonard Wood, a friend of Roosevelt. (City of Las Vegas Museum and Rough Rider Memorial Collection, 2012.11.18)

Roosevelt stands in the middle of this picture at the Hotel Castañeda, next to the rail depot, with Pueblo Indian friends he invited to the reunion. Roosevelt took great pride in his knowledge of and experience in Western states. Reminding the public of this would serve him well as he ran for national office. (DL.)

The future president leads a parade of veterans. The man next to him on the white horse is likely a member of the Grand Army of the Republic (GAR). The GAR was a fraternal organization of veterans of the Union army in the Civil War. Following the two are Rough Riders from the recent Spanish-American War. (JH.)

The Rough Riders parade before the assembled Las Vegas crowds during the first Rough Rider reunion. Although the Spanish-American war was short, it was a popular conflict. The news media painted Spain as a swaggering tyrannical power that oppressed its colonies in Cuba and the Philippines. When the US battleship *Maine* blew up in Havana harbor, few expressed doubt that Spain was responsible. (CLLV.)

Col. Theodore Roosevelt sat with some of his officers for this studio portrait during the first Rough Rider reunion held in Las Vegas. Roosevelt and his Rough Riders were among those responsible for the victory at the Battle of San Juan Hill in Cuba. The battle was the most famous of the Spanish-American War. (City of Las Vegas Museum and Rough Rider Memorial Collection, 65.34.2)

An important part of the Las Vegas economy was servicing the railroad. Until the approach of the railroad, timbers in the mountains had gone relatively unused. Then, suddenly, they were in great demand. Town merchants contributed to building this plant, which treated timbers for use as ties. The treated and uniform ties, called sleepers in Britain, supported the steel rails. (FB.)

This is the original Las Vegas Railroad Depot. It served as the town's train station until the Santa Fe Railroad built the present depot and the Castañeda Hotel. The photograph is from the 1880s or 1890s. Though the occasion is unknown, it must have been a momentous one, judging from the crowd. (City of Las Vegas Museum and Rough Rider Memorial Collection, 2010.13.1.)

The first El Porvenir Hotel, shown here, built in 1893, burned down in 1903. It was called El Cerro de la Escondida (Spanish for "Hidden Hill") but was renamed El Porvenir, meaning "the Future" in English. The name was either to help Anglos with an easier pronunciation or for a nearby monolith, depending on the source one consults. This is a particularly fine picture of posed El Porvenir guests in late-19th-century dress. (FB.)

Missouri Valley Bridge and Iron Works of Leavenworth, Kansas, constructed this bridge in 1909. It spanned the Gallinas at Bridge Street until it was replaced by the present structure. (FB.)

The iron bridge over the Gallinas River was not for speeding across. The overhead sign warns against moving across it faster than a walk's pace. This might have been necessary to keep nervous horses under control in the confined space of the bridge. Today, the speed limit on the bridge is still a placid 15 miles per hour. The picture is from about 1900. (Dr. W.P. Mills, courtesy City of Las Vegas Museum and Rough Rider Memorial Collection, 67.9.11.)

This locomotive, which was working on the Santa Fe line, is very similar to the first locomotive that arrived in Las Vegas on July 4, 1879. The locomotive worked by heating water in a confined space and circulating the resulting steam to turn the wheels. By 1879, such engines were reliable, but operations were less so. Simple carelessness or operational misadventure caused a number of accidents. (LP.)

This is the Las Vegas Tigers baseball team for an unknown year, probably some time in the 1880s or 1890s. By the 1850s, baseball was the national pastime, and after the Civil War, there were professional teams in several large cities. Las Vegas was too small for professionals, of course, so the picture is no doubt of men who just enjoyed playing. (City of Las Vegas Museum and Rough Rider Memorial Collection, 62.47.5.)

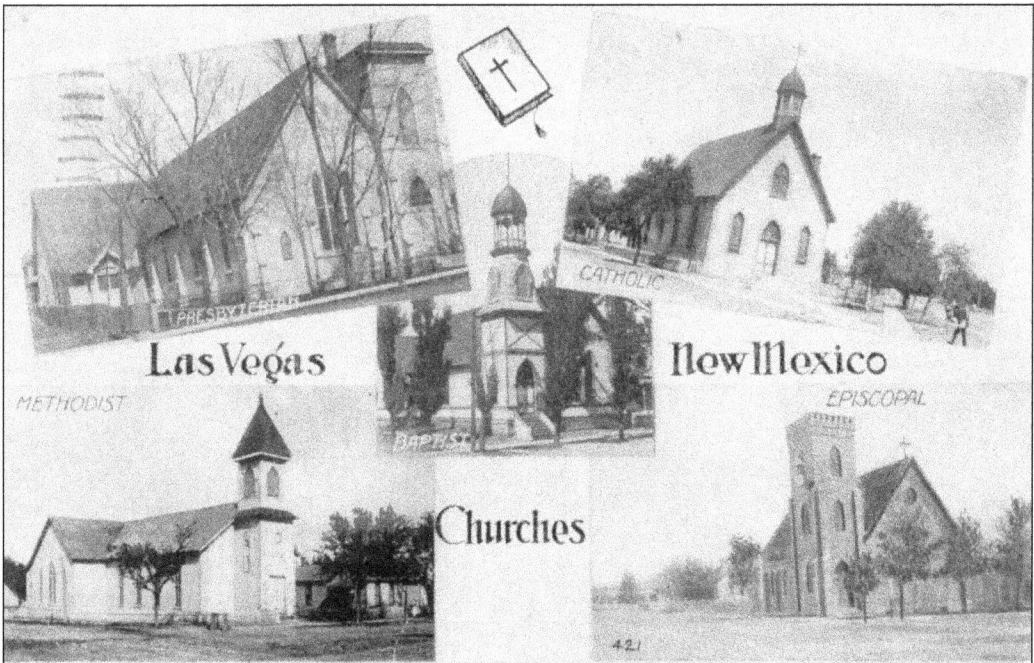

This postcard depicts some of the early Las Vegas churches. Catholics built their first church, Our Lady of Sorrows, in 1836. Presbyterians started a church with nine members in 1870. The Methodist church organized in 1879. Peace Episcopal was also established that year. (City of Las Vegas Museum and Rough Rider Memorial Collection, 64.3.3.)

These Las Vegas men used their hand-powered car to get to work sites on the Santa Fe Railroad in the 1880s and 1890s, the early days of operations. Railroads today still use small cars for inspecting track and performing maintenance, but they travel to work sites without the need for hand cranking. This crew was near Roy at the time of the photograph. (RL.)

A crew at *La Voz del Pueblo* pauses from work to pose some time in the 1880s or 1890s. Notice the segmented boxes for holding different type in the shape of the alphabet letters and the hammer for pounding the type into forms for the printed pages. (OLOS.)

According to its label, this is a view of the Las Vegas "school district" in 1900. It shows the town from the Presbyterian mission eastward. At the far right edge is New Mexico Normal University with Springer Hall. The Plaza with its big, shady trees dominates the middle and left center of the picture. (BD.)

The ornate fireplace at the Montezuma Hotel, seen here as it appeared in 1886, must have been one of the most striking features for arriving guests. The fireplace is still one of the most eye-catching features of the main building. The former Montezuma today is the campus of the Armand Hammer United World College of the American West, which is dedicated to teaching international understanding. (FB.)

A crowd gathers in the Plaza for what appears to be a race in the 1880s. The Plaza has been a focal point for events in the area from the beginning of Las Vegas until the present time. Today, lofty trees planted many years ago shade the Plaza, and it has a gazebo for speeches and musical performances. It has been the scene of numerous motion pictures, including 1968's *Easy Rider*. (FB.)

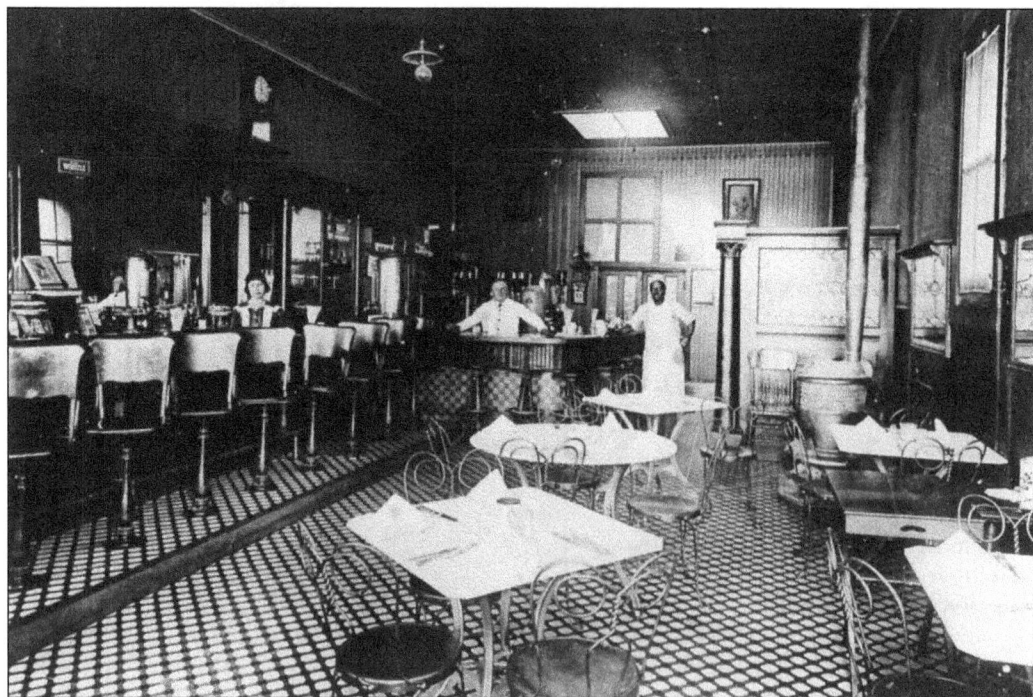

The date of this picture appears to be some time before 1900. There is a stove to warm customers in winter and three people ready to meet any needs at this café on Railroad Avenue; however, those wire-backed chairs certainly look uncomfortable. (OLOS.)

Two

THE 20TH CENTURY BEGINS

The nation turned its eyes to Las Vegas in 1912 for a world heavyweight boxing match. The national news media covered the match with a level of racism that is difficult to imagine a little over a century later. When Jack Johnson, a black man, won the championship over James J. Jeffries, a white man, in 1910, riots broke out in 50 cities. Even the *New York Times* called for a "Great White Hope" to set things right. This image was captured during the defending champion's arrival in Las Vegas to fight Jim Flynn. (TS.)

Jack Johnson and his party lined up for this group shot before the heavyweight fight at their training camp in Montezuma. Jackson's nickname was the "Galveston Giant" for his birthplace in Texas. He is the subject of the 1970 movie *The Great White Hope*, starring James Earl Jones, as well as the Ken Burns documentary *Unforgivable Blackness: The Rise and Fall of Jack Johnson.* Burns based his documentary on a book of the same name by Geoffrey C. Ward. (DL.)

Jack Johnson prepares for the heavyweight fight by practicing with his sparring partner. Before 1908, there had been two separate heavyweight championship titles: one white, one black. After two years of stalking the reigning world champion, Tommy Burns, Johnson succeeded in getting a match with him in 1908 and winning after 14 rounds. (OLOS.)

The new champion created caused more controversy by refusing to comply with "race mixing." Here, he relaxes in Las Vegas with his fiancée, Irene Pineau, whom he would marry later in 1912, before the match. Johnson's marriage to Pineau led to his conviction under the Mann Act, which outlawed bringing a woman across state lines for immoral purposes, but prosecutors also interpreted it to criminalize relationships between black men and white women. (DL.)

Jim Flynn arrived in Las Vegas with his party on May 9, 1912. He was a New Jersey native, and when the match with Johnson took place in Las Vegas, he had been boxing professionally for 13 years. After the fight, he continued to box another 10 years. He died 10 years after his retirement. (DL.)

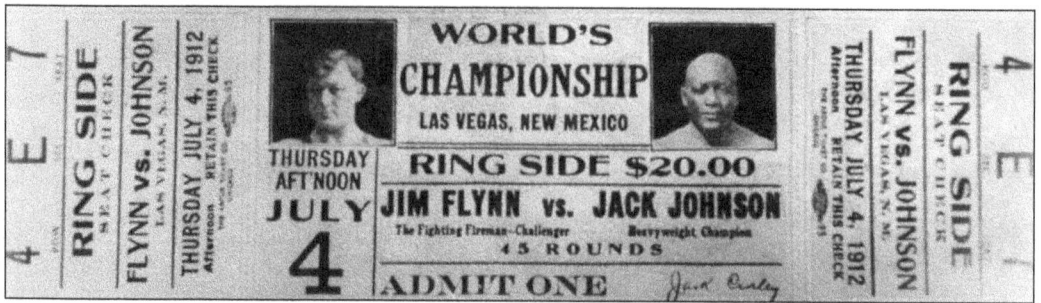

Responding to protests against brutality of boxing, the governor threatened to bar the match, so tickets like this sold sluggishly. Promoters were barely able to pay the boxers after Johnson won. The referee, who was in this case a sheriff, called the fight by a technical knockout when challenger Flynn persisted with head butts. Thus Johnson retained the title. He kept it until 1915, when he was finally defeated. (FB.)

This is the new century's method of traveling with a baby into and out of the back country. With two men to make sure there are no mishaps along the way, the trip to or from Las Vegas to the mountain resort should be uneventful. Even the very young contributed to the area's economy when the mountain resorts attracted tourists. (FD.)

The first airplane to stay for long in Las Vegas was for use in a movie. Romaine Fielding, an early movie star and producer, made several films in Las Vegas, including a major motion picture by the standards of the time. *The Golden God* of 1913 was the most expensive movie of its day and involved hundreds of extras. A battle scene filmed in west Las Vegas featured this biplane dropping fake bombs on extras. (LP.)

In recent years, the motion picture industry has provided employment to many New Mexico residents who work as extras for movies in the state, with many filmed in Las Vegas. The industry follows a long tradition. This 1913 crowd is all extras for Romaine Fielding's *The Golden God*. Sadly, the print for the movie was lost in a fire, and no copies survive. Fielding took over the Plaza Hotel for his studio, and a sign painted on the side of the building advertising that fact is still visible. (LP.)

This Victorian house, probably situated on Railroad Avenue, was home to an employee of the railroad who needed to be near work. It dates from the early 1900s. (DL.)

This is the sitting room of El Porvenir Resort, decorated in true Southwest style, which offers a place to sit for every comfort level from soft to hard and with or without an ottoman. The timbers on the ceiling are vigas and probably extend through the wall and outside. (City of Las Vegas Museum and Rough Rider Memorial Collection, 2008.19.1.)

These are likely guests at Montezuma or El Porvenir off for a picnic. The women standing all wear shirtwaists. The Montgomery Ward 1895 catalog said that the clothing items are "the correct thing for general wear and are by far the most becoming and sensible article of women's attire to receive fashion's universal approval." A woman could wear a shirtwaist over an "old dress skirt" to provide "a cool, comfortable and up-to-date- costume that will quite astonish you." (DL.)

Late-19th-century women like these would never think of exposing their limbs (or using such rude terms as arms or legs). Even on an outing into the mountains for a picnic, women wore long skirts and men donned ties. While they may look formal, there is no doubt they were enjoying themselves. Such excursions as these from their hotels—the Montezuma or El Porvenir, perhaps—brought welcome money to the Las Vegas economy. (DL.)

Las Vegas merchant Margarito Romero built El Porvenir Resort at the foot of Hermit Peak. He may have done so to be with his friend Giovanni Maria de Augustino, the hermit who lived on the peak for several years. This picture shows the good fortune symbol on the building's facade often hidden in photographic shadows. Unfortunately, it has come to be recognized for tragic reasons as a swastika (LB.)

El Porvenir Resort charged guests $7 a week for accommodations and amenities. It offered the use of rowboats, and guests like these could enjoy burros for trail outings. A commissary on the grounds provided food, but there was no dining room, as cooking hot meals proved not profitable. Guests, however, could arrange for food delivery from Las Vegas. (DL.)

El Porvenir included 480 acres of land and this artificial lake. The mountain in the background is Hermit Peak, which is 10,259 feet (3,127 meters) high. It is about 15 miles northwest of Las Vegas. The peak resembles the face of a man from a distance. Pueblo tribes held the peak to be sacred. "The Great Spirit," they said, "is present in all mountains. Only in this one does He reveal His face." (DL.)

The 1920 lobby of El Porvenir Resort had decorative appointments in Santa Fe style long before the term became fashionable. Rugs are everywhere—on the floor, on the coffee table, on the couch, and on the wall. It appears that at least one might be a Navajo rug and, if so, would have deserved better care. Navajo rugs should be displayed using frames that do not fray or stretch the cloth. (City of Las Vegas Museum and Rough Rider Memorial Collection, 2011.2.244.)

A camping party at El Porvenir is photographed about 1915 with Hermit Peak in the background. Many call the mountain Hermit's Peak, but the official name is Hermit Peak, according to the US Board on Geographic Names. The hermit arrived in the Las Vegas area in 1863 and left in 1867. After his departure, pilgrims climbed to the hut on the mountain's summit in which he had once lived. These pilgrimages continued for many years after the hermit's death. (DL.)

This man out for a buggy ride is pictured at the rear of the synagogue on Douglas Avenue. On the hill above is Douglas School. The school system razed the school in 1926, so the picture dates from that year or earlier. (DL.)

Ralph Emerson Twitchell came to Las Vegas in 1882 and worked in the law office of a solicitor for the Santa Fe Railway. Later, he was mayor of Santa Fe and judge advocate of the territorial militia, in which he received the rank of colonel. He enjoyed that title and kept it the rest of his life. His five-volume *Leading Facts of New Mexican History* is a major contribution to the state's annals. (DL.)

The Las Vegas Railroad Yard was south of where the Amtrak station is today. The yard was a working area. There must have been noise all through the day and long into the night as men assembled, disassembled, and repaired the train cars. Las Vegas was a division point, so trips for crews began and ended here. Numerous railroad families made their homes in town. (LP.)

Las Vegas was a busy rail center in the first decades of the 20th century. The Santa Fe Railway's tie-making plant and roundhouse employed many in Las Vegas, and the activities of its workers and their organizations drew visitors to the area. A ball held by the Brotherhood of Locomotive Firemen in 1903 at the hot springs drew people from as far away as Albuquerque. This is a group of Santa Fe Railroad workers from Las Vegas in 1911. (FB.)

The Santa Fe Depot, built in the Mission style in 1900, has changed little today. This is what the depot looked like in about 1915. In addition to freight trains stopping in Las Vegas, the depot had several passenger train arrivals and departures daily. (OLOS.)

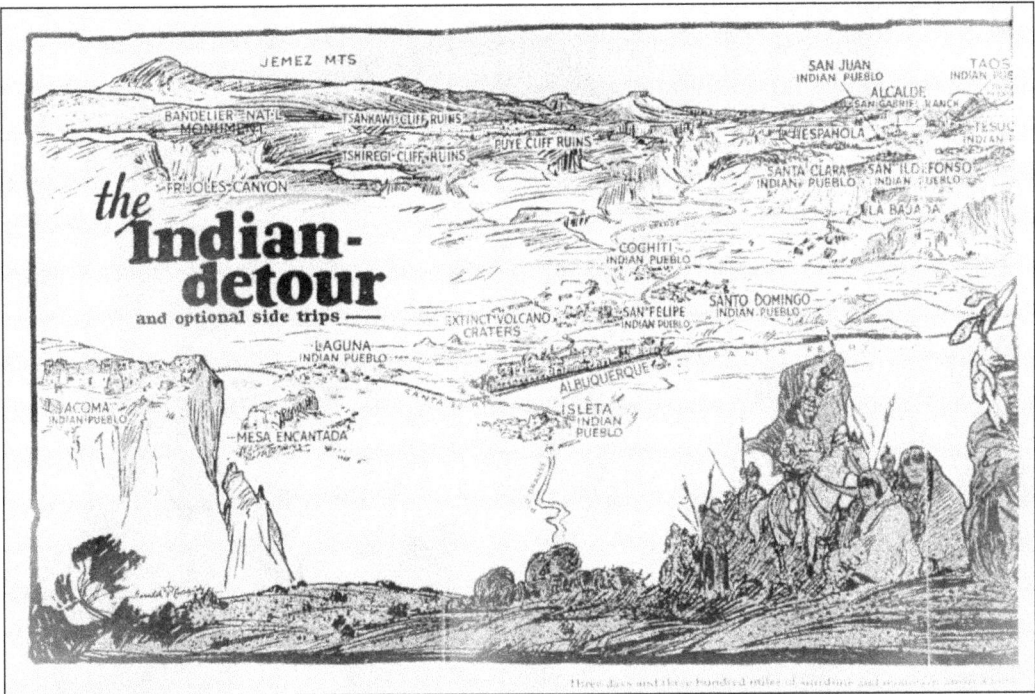

Westbound rail passengers could leave their train at Las Vegas for a trip by coach into exotic Indian country. The map on this page shows some of the attractions tourists could view by coach before they resumed their rail journey in Albuquerque or Arizona. The Fred Harvey Company operated Indian Detours from the Castañeda Hotel in Las Vegas to its sister hotel, the Alvarado in Albuquerque. (DL.)

Eastbound travelers could take their Indian Detour trip by leaving the train at Albuquerque and reboarding at Las Vegas. It was an opportunity for travelers to see a part of the country that was considered exotic. The landscape was unfamiliar desert instead of green and lush, and the people lived in ways that were more foreign still, coexisting in small villages and speaking unfamiliar languages. (DL.)

The wool industry was a major source of income in the Las Vegas area for many years. This Las Vegas roller mill processed wool to remove extraneous matter. Roller mills are something like giant carding operations that both clean the wool and straighten the fibers. After aligning, the fibers are suitable for various applications, such as yarn. (ILV.)

Two gentlemen and a lady prepare to set out on an expedition from El Porvenir Resort while a child watches from behind. The photographer caught these three aboard their burros about 1900. Note the resplendent mustache and sideburns on the man at the far right. (DL.)

These carts on Railroad Avenue are full of wool and waiting to be unloaded. Production of wool was once so extensive that wool carts like these sometimes lined up as far as Romeroville, five miles away, to unload in town. The Brown and Manzanares Company, on the left, is in a structure constructed between 1898 and 1902. Today, it is Hays Plumbing and Heating. (OLOS.)

Agriculture was the purpose of Storrie Dam, built in the late 1920s by San Francisco contractor R.C. Storrie. However, farmers who bought land around it and used its water for their crops were unable to make money due to the weather, transportation costs, and the Great Depression. Eventually, the development reorganized under the Storrie Project Water Users Association, which still exists today. Storrie Lake State Park uses the body of water and its surroundings for recreation. (LP.)

This is a view of Bridge Street in 1904 looking west towards old town. The car to the right is turning onto the branch line that ran along the bank of the Gallinas River and out to Montezuma. The other car is going to or coming from the Plaza. (FB.)

Street Scene, Las Vegas, N. Mex.

A postcard manufacturer chose this picture of Douglas Avenue in 1914 to typify Las Vegas. At this time, the Las Vegas Transit Company, a subsidiary of the Las Vegas Light and Power Company, operated the trolley. In another 13 years, it would cease operations, giving way to the power of the automobile. (OLOS.)

Pictured is a typing class at New Mexico Normal University about 1910. It is hard to ignore that there are there are only women at the machines, as no male would ever consider learning to type at this time. Such a skill was fitting only for a woman, which she would employ as a secretary or a similar position. (DL.)

A 1912 fire destroyed the historic Buffalo Bar, formerly called the Exchange Hotel, and also damaged the Romero mercantile buildings on the south side of the Plaza. The written notation reads, "Danzinger and Romero Bldg's after the fire 6-8-12." The Buffalo Bar had briefly been the New Mexico Territory capitol during the Confederate invasion; it was in the empty space at the right of the picture, now occupied by the Las Vegas Police. (FB.)

The E. Romero Hose and Fire Company takes a practice run at the Plaza Hotel about 1917. Notice the men were able to reach all floors of the hotel. This is an ability not possessed by municipal fire departments these days. Also, note the ornate iron railings on the first-floor balcony. (FB.)

This group photograph shows the E. Romero Hose and Fire Company in front of the company's firehouse, which still exists today, housing a business on Bridge Street. This photograph is from about 1905, twenty-three years after the founding of the company in 1882, as the sign on the building states. The Romero Company firefighters are now in a modern building on New Mexico Avenue near the county courthouse. (OLOS.)

In 1916, the E. Romero Hose and Fire Company sold its horses and bought two LaFrance fire trucks. Here, members of the company pose proudly with their new engines. A group of Roma (or gypsies) acquired the retired horses. At the first fire alarm following the sale, the faithful animals raced back to the station house, billowing tents and outraged new owners in their wake. (OLOS.)

Fire companies No. 1 (East Las Vegas) on the left and E. Romero Hose and Fire Company (of old Las Vegas) on the right show off their new LaFrance fire trucks in 1916. They pose in front of the Coronado Theater on Sixth Street where Gamble's Hardware now stands. (OLOS.)

The 21st century provides people with innumerable ways to entertain themselves, with almost more ways to fill time than they can handle. A hundred years ago, the situation was quite different. Back then, it was often difficult to find ways to occupy time. One of the ways to have fun and get together for conversation at the turn of the 20th century was a quilting party, like the one pictured here. (DL.)

The picture has an old caption that reads, "In back of Dr. Rice's home;" however, neither of these people seems old enough to have earned a medical certificate, so Dr. Rice is ruled out as one of them. The happy but unidentified couple appears pleased to have a stack of wood ready for the winter. (DL.)

This is a group of well-dressed young ladies and gentlemen from the first decade of the 20th century. The boys in front wear shorts and stockings. It would be a few more years before they will be old enough to wear full-length trousers. Many of the girls seem restless. Perhaps they have tired of waiting for the photographer to finish and want the ordeal to be over. The stern-looking man in back ensures no one will leave prematurely. (CT.)

This unidentified couple gazes confidently into the future from the early 1900s. She wears a bonnet, lace collar, and many ruffles, while he is in neckerchief, coat, vest, and striped trousers, and his hat rests on his knee. Clearly, they have worn their best for this studio portrait. How many citizens of Las Vegas can proudly claim them as ancestors today? (City of Las Vegas Museum and Rough Rider Memorial Collection, 62.35.4.)

This picture, taken in the early years of the 20th century, is of Ramon Lujan and Hileria Gonzales de Lujan. From their faces, it is clear this couple has seen and heard much during their years on earth. They both gaze into the camera with steady expressions, neither smiling nor downcast. (RR.)

Browne and Manzanares was located on Railroad Avenue. This ad offers an idea of what they stocked. Several merchants in Las Vegas specialized in supplying farmers and ranchers with equipment. The business's marketing area was vast, extending well to the east and northeast. Santa Fe and Albuquerque were the only major competition to the west and southwest, and in those days, both of those towns were many hours away. (LVO.)

This crowd gathers in 1920s for an Independence Day parade at Douglas and Railroad Avenues. Almost everyone has automobiles, but a few holdouts drove to town with horses. The building on the right just past the saloon was the boardinghouse for Harvey Girls. Harvey Girls were employees of the Fred Harvey Company, which operated hotels, dining rooms, and dining cars along the Santa Fe Railroad. In Las Vegas, the Fred Harvey Company operated the Castañeda Hotel and Montezuma Resort. (FL.)

In this image of Douglas and Sixth Streets, a crowd has congregated in the intersection, though the reason is unknown. There are signs advertising jewelry, meat, grocery, and a bakery. It seems Douglas Avenue was a much busier place than it is today. (City of Las Vegas Museum and Rough Rider Memorial Collection, 76.4.31.)

ILFELD'S "THE PLAZA"

The exterior of Charles Ilfeld's store on the Plaza is in the middle of this grouping, its interior around the edges, and the warehouse loading dock on the bottom left. This was likely an advertisement given to customers for use as a postcard. However, if made today, it would likely include a few people in the pictures to offer some scale. (ILV.)

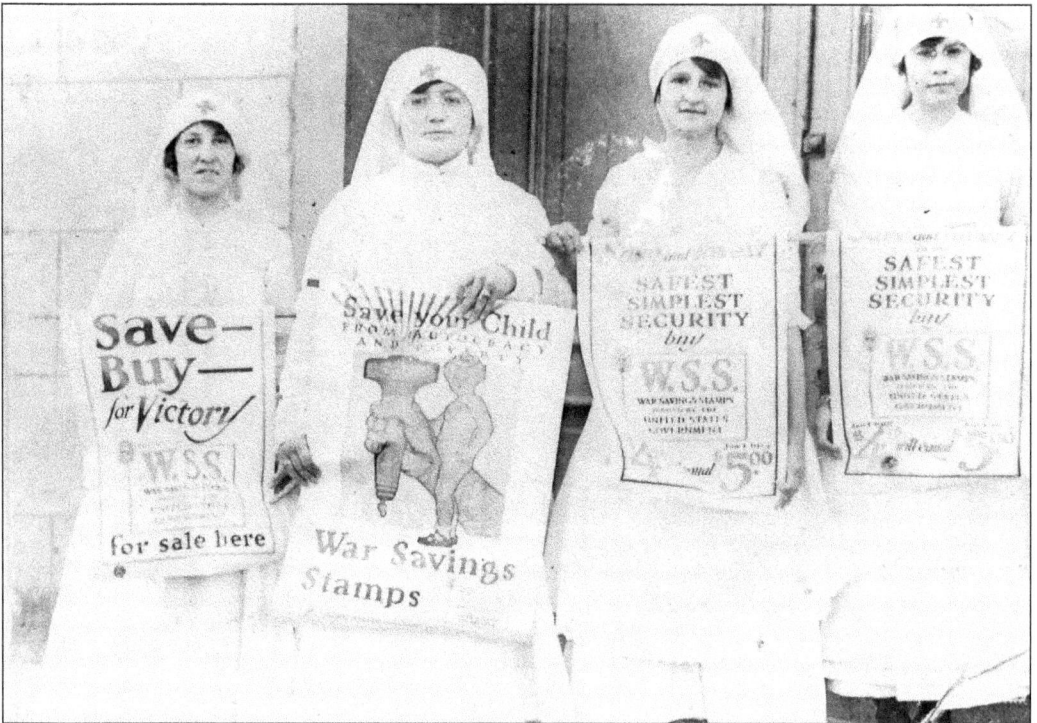

These women are out to sell savings stamps to finance the cost of World War I. One sign declares that an investment of $4.12 will earn $5 on January 1, 1923. The US government issued the stamps. The poster with a child and an arm bearing a torch tells the prospective purchaser to "Save your Child from Autocracy and Poverty." (OLOS MS.)

New Mexico Normal University fielded this football team for the 1901 season, its first year of existence. The banner is difficult to read in its entirety, but the team's record that year was clearly a rout. It beat the University of Texas, the University of New Mexico, possibly Brigham Young University, and what may be Agriculture and Mechanical Arts. The team allowed none of its opponents to score points at all. (DL.)

New Mexico Normal University students were probably engaging in a fraternity initiation in this picture; either that, or the work-study program must have found it difficult to recruit male participants. (DL.)

This building was the New Mexico Territory's insane asylum on Hot Springs Boulevard. The treatment of mental conditions continues to be a significant source of employment in Las Vegas. A large campus on Hot Springs Boulevard has grown from the building in this picture. (JH.)

A National Guard band practices marching in this photograph taken during World War I at Camp Luna. Only one permanent building is visible, and the remainder of the accommodations are tents. It is likely that the picture dates from the early months of the war, when the nation was gearing up to send troops overseas. (LP.)

The interior of the Gross, Kelly Company's Las Vegas headquarters is pictured about 1905. Gross, Kelly was a wholesale/retail firm. Notice the vault on the rear wall, guarded by a bison head. This is the firm's inner office, as the left wall consists of teller windows. (LP.)

In 1903, a bill passed the state legislature that provided for a public wagon road between the courthouses in Santa Fe and Las Vegas. According to the bill, the road "shall be constructed over the most feasible route through or near the canyon of the Santa Fe River . . . over the mountain range at the most practical route to the east of said city." In June that year, work began on the eastern side of the route in Gallinas Canyon. This picture is from about 1920. (TG.)

The state assigned 25 convicts from the penitentiary in Santa Fe to the task of the public wagon road. By 1907, the road was within a mile of the Santa Fe National Forest boundary when the appropriation money ran out. The road project never gained support for completion. For the time, it was ambitious work, as this picture taken about 1920 suggests. (TG.)

Bridge Street wears decorations for Independence Day in this photograph; however, the year is unknown. The street is unpaved, but it has trolley tracks. There is a wooden sidewalk with a ramp to help ease the rise from one level to another. In the distance, a wagon and team are visible, but it is not possible to determine what animals are involved. (FB.)

The date of this picture is unknown, but it is clearly a furniture repair and upholstering shop. One man works on a rocking chair as the man nearest the camera focuses on upholstery. (FB.)

Sometimes things go terribly wrong with machines. They are created to save time or effort, but occasionally, they malfunction due to human error or unforeseen difficulties with the mechanics involved. This locomotive, which blew up somewhere near Las Vegas, is an example of how engines do not need to be complex to fail spectacularly. (FB.)

The daughter of Ezequiel Cabeza De Baca christens the USS *New Mexico*. Her father, who was born in Las Vegas, was New Mexico's second state governor under the US government and the first of Hispanic heritage. The launching date was April 23, 1917. The *New Mexico* was active during World War II and was decommissioned in 1946. (FB.)

For the Las Vegas centennial in 1905, the Gross, Kelly Company, a retail/wholesale firm, crafted this parade float. The buildings in diminishing sizes represent the company's Las Vegas headquarters and its branches in Albuquerque, Trinidad, Tucumcari, Pecos, Logan in Quay County, and Epris in Guadalupe County. (PSLV.)

Someone has written in Spanish on this early-20th-century photograph that it is "Rapid Express Distribution." It is not much different than it would have been a hundred years earlier. (OLOS JD.)

This c. 1910 picture shows construction of a dam to impound water for harvesting ice during the winter in Gallinas Canyon. It was one of eight such ice ponds owned by the Agua Pura Company. Ice harvesting was a major economic force in Las Vegas for many years. (DL.)

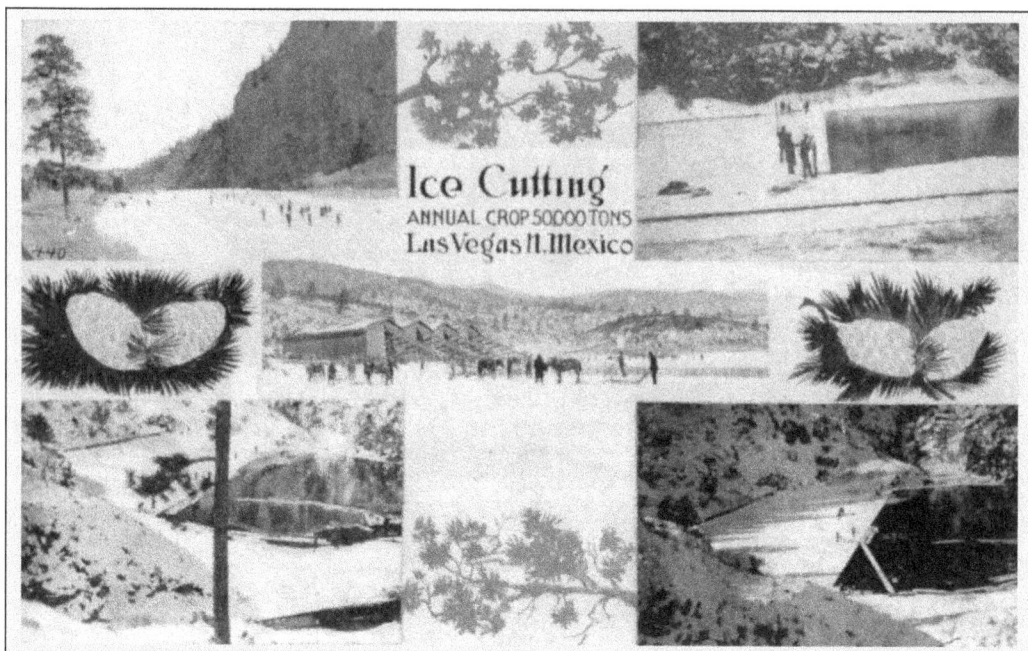

This postcard from about 1910 shows several aspects of ice cutting at the ponds just beyond the hot springs in Gallinas Canyon. Until the introduction of refrigeration, the use of ice for food preservation was a major source of income for many in the Las Vegas area, thanks to the cliffs that kept the ponds in the shadows for long hours during the winter. (City of Las Vegas Museum and Rough Rider Memorial Collection, 200.5.)

Horse-drawn saws cut ice on the Gallinas Canyon ponds in this c. 1900 picture. Notice a block of ice halfway up the ramp leading to the railcars parked above the pond. (FB.)

The ponds were also used for recreation, as seen in this picture from about 1920. Note the wooden flume along the cliffs. This was to deliver drinking water to Las Vegas, bypassing the nine dams and eight ice ponds. To construct it, laborers had to crawl along the heights on 10-inch planks supported by spikes driven into holes drilled into the granite wall. The skating pond is featured in the 2009 film *Brothers*. (FL.)

In the early 20th century, S. Omar Barker (not related to the author), pictured here with a deceased mountain lion, was starting a remarkable career. After graduation from the normal university, he taught Spanish in Las Vegas, fought in World War I, taught English, served in the state legislature, and then took up a career as full-time freelance writer. He turned out 1,500 short stories and novelettes, around 1,200 articles, and 2,000 poems. His unofficial title was New Mexico's "Poet Lariat." (DL.)

In 1910, the Plaza still had streetcar tracks, and its trees had obtained a respectable size. There are stone curbs and sidewalks, but the street remained unpaved until 1920. A bandstand is in the middle of the Plaza for musical performances and speeches. The large buildings in the distance are the Plaza Hotel on the left and the Charles Ilfeld Company on the right. (OLOS.)

In this 1915 picture are the Plaza Hotel and a Model T horseless carriage. In 1899, Las Vegas saw its first automobile owner. The machine came from Trinidad, Colorado, and was bought by a Santa Fe Railroad engineer. He drove it south while accompanied by a Trinidad mechanic. Having the mechanic along was an advantage. There were only dirt roads in those days outside big cities. They consisted of little more than parallel ruts; tires blew out regularly, as did car engines. (LP.)

S. Omar Barker was not the only talented member of his family. His wife, Elsa, shown here, was a writer of many Western novels. The public saw only her initials and last name on the novels, however. While Westerns were very popular at the time, publishing executives thought the readership would never accept such books if written by a female. (DL.)

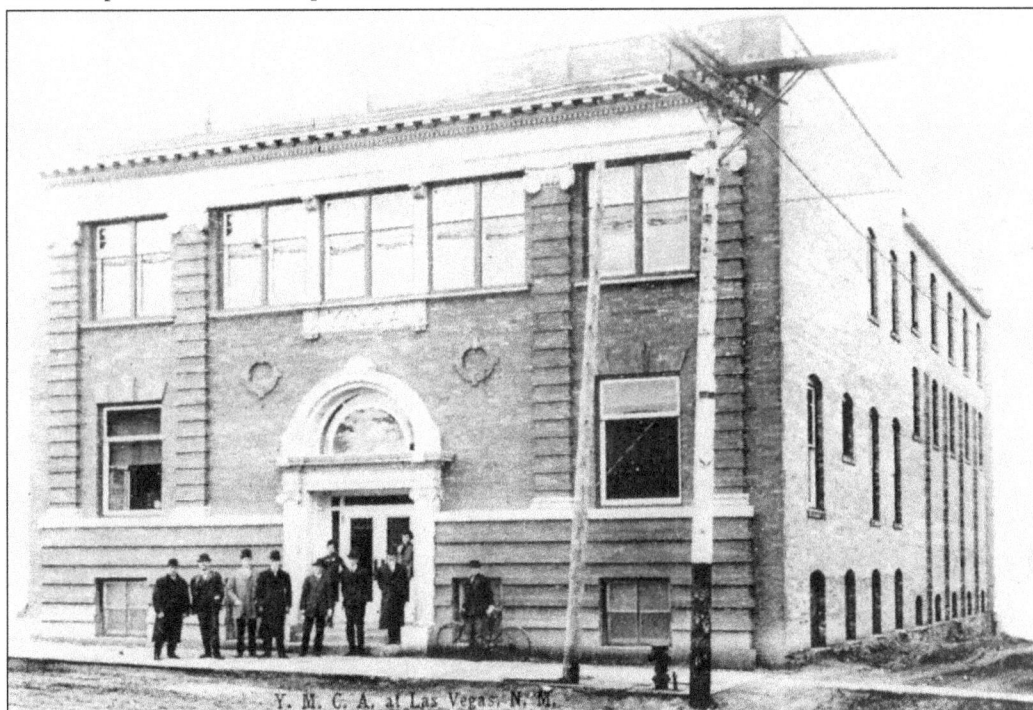

In 1903, the Young Men's Christian Association (YMCA) began a drive to build a local facility. Two years later, construction began. The building had a small gym, swimming pool, reading room, and 16 guest rooms. The Y taught swim and gym classes in the building, organized local athletic teams, and coached football and basketball teams. It lost money during World War II and closed shortly thereafter. (FB.)

This is Castle High School in about 1915. It took its name from the structure's crenellated walls. The school system had it torn down in 1976. (OLOS.)

The ad on the side of this Wells Fargo delivery wagon at Douglas Avenue and Sixth Street promotes speedy holiday delivery in about 1900. The Murphy Drugs building is now Community First Bank. (OLOS PC.)

Normal University, Las Vegas, N. M.

Pictured in this 1900 postcard is Springer Hall, which honors Maxwell Land Grant Company attorney and normal university regent Frank Springer. The university constructed it in 1898, but the building was damaged by fire in 1922. Springer received a full restoration to its original exterior appearance, with the exception of simpler window frames. In 1955, another fire severely damaged the building, so the university demolished it. (OLOS.)

The Springer Hall fire of 1922 caused considerable damage but did not destroy the structure. It was repaired and used for another 33 years. (DL.)

Plaza Garage stood on South Pacific Street near the Plaza. This is where automobile owners knew to go when their horseless carriages stopped running. The customers could get some lunch—cold drinks and 5¢ hamburgers—while waiting for the repairs. It also appears that the garage could arrange for overnight accommodations at Plaza Camp (this was before motels). (DL.)

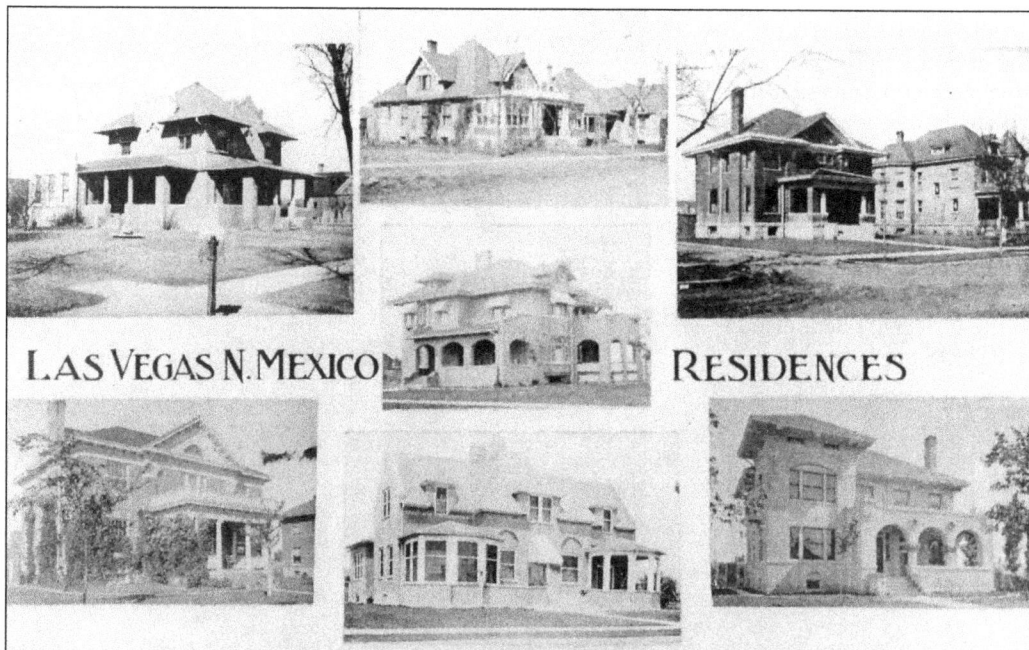

This postcard sports a selection of the town's celebrated heritage of large, comfortable homes built, for the most part, with railroad and wool money. The wealth of these houses has provided moviemakers with a number of film sets, such as the 1993 Warner Bros. picture *Wyatt Earp*, starring Kevin Costner; the porch of a house on Jackson Street near Eighth Street was used for one scene. (RR.)

This picture may not look much like the Las Vegas area, but it is. This is a lettuce field around Storrie Reservoir about 1925. As noted on page 61, agriculture was the reservoir's primary purpose. Some seasons, the crops were good, but at other times, the weather was not cooperative. It appears that this photograph is from one of the better years. (LP.)

This couple takes in the air at Montezuma Hotel around 1900. The lady sits sidesaddle in keeping with the etiquette of the time. The man wears a bowler with a high crown. Behind them is the hotel's casino building. (DL.)

This is a c. 1900 image of the Presbyterian mission, which was established in 1891. Located near the Plaza, the building has recently returned to service in its original purpose. (DL.)

This is an exceptionally fine family portrait from around 1914. The eight people range in age from very young to elderly. The only things known about this family are their surname, Benavediz, and that they lived somewhere in the Las Vegas area in an adobe dwelling. (OLOS.)

Residents of Las Vegas enjoyed games and sports in the early years of the 20th century. Various sports teams represented local high schools, churches, the YMCA, and the normal university (later New Mexico Highlands). This undated picture of the normal university baseball team is possibly from the 1910s. (DL.)

This is the 1906 Las Vegas High School Cardinals football team. The two men in ties at the far left and far right in the back row appear to be teachers and coaches. Neither seems much older than the team members themselves. (City of Las Vegas Museum and Rough Rider Memorial Collection, 2010.1.181.)

These New Mexico Normal University students have been playing a rousing game of tennis in about 1910. They have gone to the extreme of rolling their sleeves up and flouting all conventions of the time. (DL.)

This languid group is the Las Vegas High School basketball team for 1912–1913. (FD.)

The Las Vegas Elks Club on Douglas Avenue, seen as this architect's drawing on a 1906 postcard, appears to have been a striking building. It burned in 1997. The blaze seems to have started in a pile of boards outside the rear of the building along the alley on its south side. It spread from the ground floor and up an open stairwell to the roof. (OLOS.)

The Duncan Opera House and Masonic Temple dominated the northeast corner of Sixth Street and Douglas Avenue in the early 1900s. The opera house space is now occupied by a drive-through bank. The Masonic temple remains. (FB.)

This is *La Voz del Pueblo*'s newspaper office and print shop in 1900. The paper was founded in the late 1890s and supported Populist or Democratic candidates against the Republicans that were favored by the *Daily Optic*. (FB.)

The *Daily Optic*'s office and print shop on Grand Avenue is seen as it looked in 1900. The *Optic* is the only local paper still in publication. The Las Vegas public could access 40 papers, including 8 dailies, in town between 1879 and 1912. Nine of them affiliated with politicians. The highest bidder could buy many of the others. (Dr. W.P. Mills, courtesy City of Las Vegas Museum and Rough Rider Memorial Collection, 67.9.14.)

Seen in the background is the town library when it was new, some time around 1900. The photographer was clearly more interested in the kids and their burro. The saplings in the picture are now mature trees around the Carnegie Library. Architects designed the library to resemble Thomas Jefferson's home, Monticello, in Charlottesville, Virginia. (DL.)

Here is another view of Carnegie Library from about 1900. The Las Vegas Carnegie Library was the first of its kind in the territory. It is also the last Carnegie Library still operating in the state. Philanthropist Andrew Carnegie donated the libraries to communities around the nation. They, in turn, agreed to provide land and operating budgets for the gifts. (Dr. W.P. Mills, courtesy City of Las Vegas Museum and Rough Rider Memorial Collection, 67.9.52.)

City planners elsewhere remarked on East Las Vegas City Hall for having civic offices and a firefighting company (which used the arched entrance) in the same building. The building in this c. 1915 photograph still stands. (LVO.)

Plastic cards (if they had been in existence) would not have been accepted in this grocery store on Bridge Street around 1920. The sign above the scales on the right reads, "No Credit." However, cash was readily accepted in exchange for items such as canned goods, candy, soda pop, and aspirin. (LVO.)

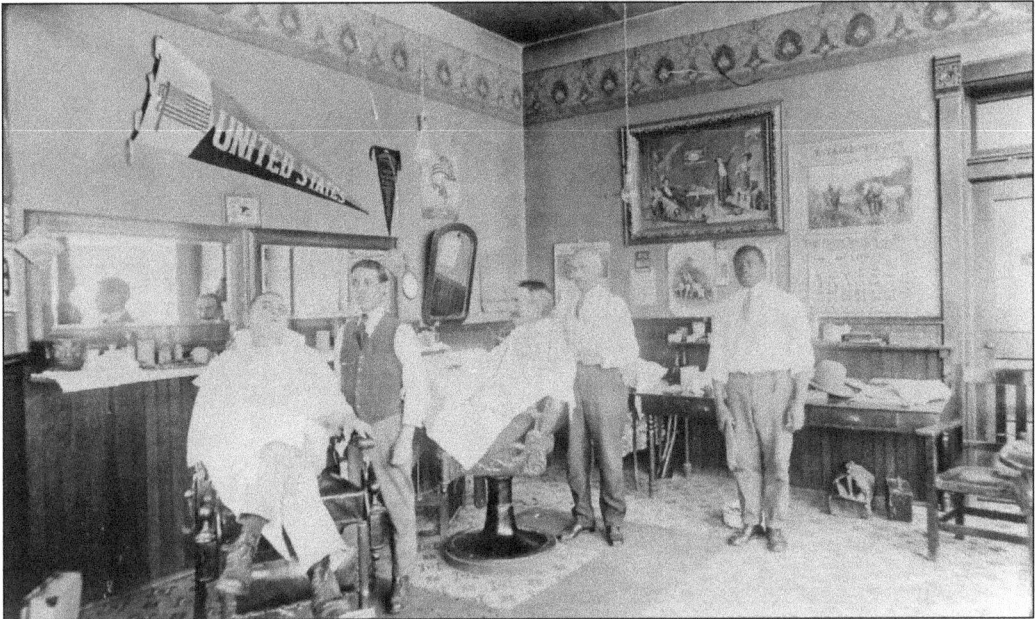

It is clear the photographer visited this barbershop in Montezuma some time during October 1919, as the barbers have a First National Bank of Las Vegas calendar in the shot that is open to that month. Note the US flag pennant and drawing of Uncle Sam holding the nation's flag along with a plaque proclaiming this is a union shop. The picture next to the calendar appears to be an ad for whiskey. (EB.)

In 1897, the Sisters of Charity raised funds locally for the building of St. Anthony's Sanitarium, which became a noted haven for patients suffering from tuberculosis. This postcard is from the period after 1910, as porches were a later addition to the initial construction. (City of Las Vegas Museum and Rough Rider Memorial Collection, 68.17.17.)

Ilfeld Auditorium is one of the oldest buildings on the New Mexico Highlands University campus. Construction began in 1914 and was completed in 1921. The building, made of hand-quarried local stone and brick, cost $75,000 in initial state appropriations and $40,000 in later appropriations and received substantial local donations. (DL.)

Ilfeld auditorium originally seated 990, but it now seats 727 due to renovations. Fixtures in the outer lobby include the Star of David, a tribute to the Jewish community and the Ilfeld family, who provided financial support to the building's construction. The dean of women at what was then the normal university requested shallow stairs "to teach the young ladies how to gracefully glide up the steps." (DL.)

A Wood Vender.   LAS VEGAS, N. M.

Las Vegas was dependent on wood for heating in the early decades of the 20th century. The nearby mountains provided an abundant supply, and the only things needed were people and animals, such as these, to get wood down from the high country and into homes. This postcard scene is from 1910 on Seventh or Eighth Street. (City of Las Vegas Museum and Rough Rider Memorial Collection, 66.20.1.)

This large group has gathered to witness the first airmail flight into Las Vegas, on November 11, 1933. (FB.)

Many women demurely rode sidesaddle in the early years of the 20th century. Society considered it unfeminine to sit with one leg on each side of the horse. (DL.)

Due to heavy rain, the Gallinas River went on a rampage in 1904, washing out bridges and stranding travelers for weeks. The Santa Fe Railroad twice put up train passengers for several days in Las Vegas while crews worked to repair the line. (DL.)

Fortunately, the 1904 flood did not take out the bridge connecting Las Vegas and East Las Vegas, the old and new towns. Bridge Street is in the distance. The pedestrians demonstrate the behavior of people who have lived any length of time in New Mexico—abundance of water will draw spectators. (DL.)

The 1904 Gallinas River flood drew spectators in period dress to see a river as wide as something more typical of Eastern states. This view faces the west. The largest buildings on the opposite shore are a public school (left) and the county courthouse (right). (DL.)

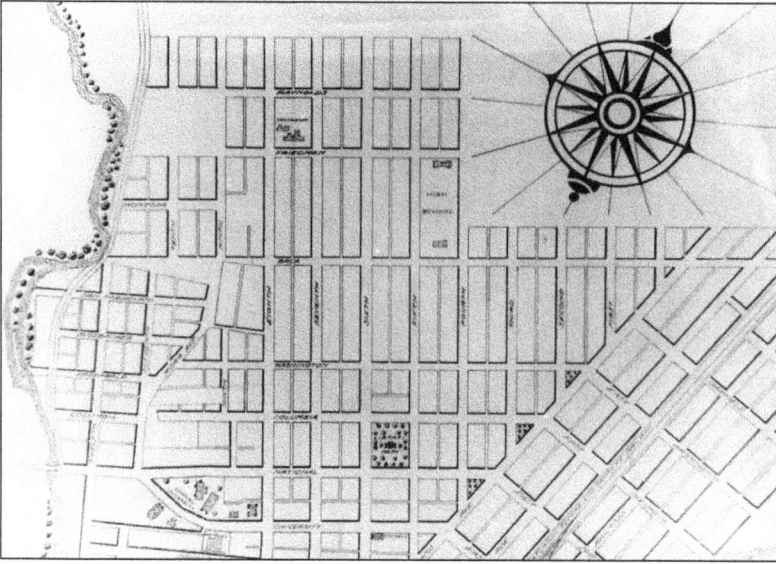

This c. 1920 map shows part of East Las Vegas. It is striking how the normal university covers an area that is considerably smaller than today's New Mexico Highlands campus. (SM.)

This is the lower part of the previous map on this page. There are few changes today compared with the features on this map. Notable is location of the old city hall. The Castañeda Hotel is labeled as "Harvey House." The Fred Harvey Company ran the Harvey House and its other hotels and dining rooms for the Santa Fe Railway. The company expected exemplary service and behavior from its employees. The Castañeda Hotel/Harvey House served as a training ground for other Harvey Company facilities around the West. (SM.)

The "Saltiest Rodeo on Earth" on this "Cowboys' Reunion" poster referred to the saltiness of a bronco, as in being very mean and wild, like the one depicted in this drawing. (FB.)

Cowboys' Reunion
Saltiest Rodeo on Earth
Las Vegas, New Mexico
July 3, 4, 5, 1928

A
$15,000
SHOW

Championship
Trophies

Official Prize List and Folder

Official Program
Cowboys Reunion
LAS VEGAS, NEW MEXICO
JULY 3, 4 & 5, 1918

Walter A. Naylor, President Cowboys Reunion Since 1915

TO THE SPECTATOR

YOU will get infinitely more enjoyment from watching the contests, if you will take the trouble to read the conditions under which they are conducted, and which are printed on the other side of this program. This is a real cowboy show, put on by real cowmen and contested by real "hands." It is a reproduction of the sports of frontier days, and retains the spirit of fair play and wholesome competition that has made western sportsmanship famous the world over. This program is handed you with the compliments of the Reunion management. The boys all want you to HAVE THE TIME OF YOUR LIFE.

This is the official program for the 1918 Cowboys Reunion. It proclaims, "This is a real cowboy show, put on by real cowmen and contested by real 'hands.' It is a reproduction of the sports of frontier days. . . . The boys all want you to HAVE THE TIME OF YOUR LIFE." (City of Las Vegas Museum and Rough Rider Memorial Collection, 73.16.41.)

99

At the 1916 Cowboys Reunion in Las Vegas, a photographer caught Walter Rummins at the instant his very salty bronco Ginn Fizz had all four legs off the ground. (AL.)

In 1906, this high-diving horse and rider thrilled the wondering crowds at the Cowboys Reunion at Gallinas Park. The essence of a thrill act was no different then than it is today; someone puts their life at risk for the excitement of others who have usually paid for the experience. (City of Las Vegas Museum and Rough Rider Memorial Collection, 2010.1.250.)

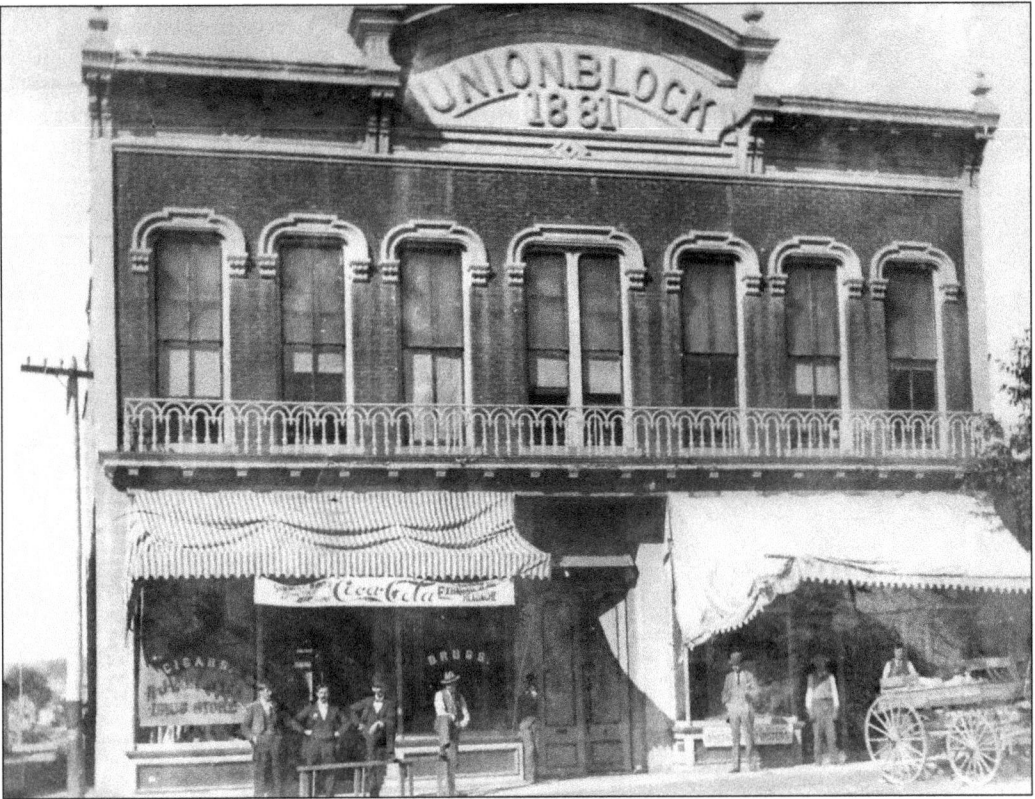

This is a c. 1913 photograph of the Union Block. The building proudly proclaims the year of its construction. First National Bank took over the block, and it is now the home of Southwest Capital Bank. (JH.)

There was an abundance of cars when the photographer set up the camera at Gallinas River Park in about 1920. The park was the site of early Las Vegas rodeos and featured a racetrack. It was located near what was then the intersection of Hot Springs Boulevard and Porter Avenue. (FL.)

Even though Fort Union didn't become a national monument until 1954, people knew it was there and were curious about it. It appears this 1930s couple obtained permission to poke around among the ruins and satisfy their urge to know more about the site. (DL.)

This 1908 shoe repair store appears to have plenty of business. Both men have their hands full at the moment, and on the right side of the picture is a bench full of completed work, which probably is waiting for customers to pick up. (OLOS.)

This is the Immaculate Conception School in 1925. The school, designed by Charles Barrett, was built in 1921 at Sixth Street and National Avenue. It is two stories high and features ornamentation of columns, urns, and arches. (JC.)

These six daring New Mexico Highlands students have crept out on the roof of Springer Hall to check out a view of the town. The camera faces west, and with luck, no one from the faculty was looking up at the time. (DL.)

Deep winter snow has long been a part of Las Vegas life. This is Sixth Street under a heavy blanket of winter precipitation some time about 1905. Moore & Jones Brothers Real Estate is the only sign that is easy to read. The firm specializes in irrigated lands but also sells livestock. There is a drugstore on that side of the street, and on the right side, it appears there is another land company in the distance; Arm Land is the firm's name. (DL.)

Three

INTO THE MID-CENTURY

This is an aerial view of Las Vegas to the northwest in the 1930s. Lincoln and Lion Parks are the empty areas closest to the camera. There is almost no development beyond the Plaza. The old Immaculate Conception Church is at University and Grand Avenues. The south side of the Douglas Avenue block between Seventh and Eighth Streets has buildings that are visible in this image. Now, the area is mostly a parking lot. The building nearest to the camera in the triangular lot at Grand, Douglas, and Seventh is gone. The structure behind it now has the "Calumet says 'Howdy' " sign left over from the filming of 1984's *Red Dawn*. (LB.)

Of the two fire companies, one serving old town and one the new, the latter company seems to have been camera shy, or perhaps the E. Romero Hose and Fire Company had better public relations advice. The Romero Company shows up in archive files quite often, but there are few pictures of the new town's firefighters. This picture from 1910 shows the Romero Company's hook and ladder team in about 1910. (FB.)

This postcard shows the side of the Castañeda Hotel facing Railroad Avenue. The other side faced the Santa Fe (now Burlington Northern Santa Fe) Railway tracks when it was new. This side of the hotel was a battle scene in the 1984 film *Red Dawn* and hosted a garden party in 1994's *Speechless*. (City of Las Vegas Museum and Rough Rider Memorial Collection, 2001.16.1.)

At Harvey's Ranch, some visitors are off to a secluded spot on El Cielo (Spanish for "the Sky") Mountain. The resort, 10,000 feet above sea level, was only accessible by using a primitive trail. Guests visited the resort to hunt turkey, deer, mountain lion, and bear. Imagine campers wearing coats and ties today. (City of Las Vegas Museum and Rough Rider Memorial Collection, 72.6.7.)

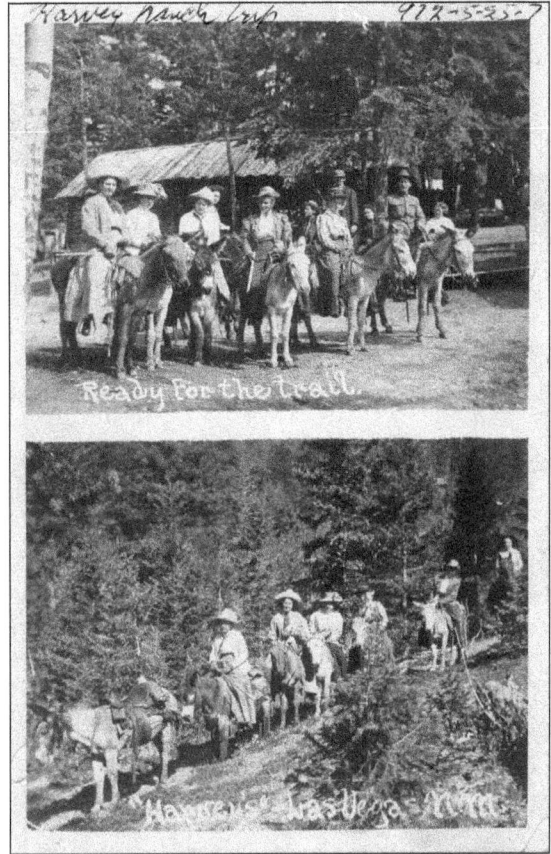

A party at Harvey's Ranch may be just arriving or homeward bound after a restful vacation in the high country. They seem dressed formally by today's standards, but it was a more formal age. (FD.)

A small group gathers by the gazebo at the Montezuma Hotel. They may have been walking in the gardens and were asked by a photographer to pose for a photograph, or they may be part of a wedding. Judging from their clothes, the image appears to have been captured some time in the 1920s. (City of Las Vegas Museum and Rough Rider Memorial Collection, 72.6.4.)

This 1920s photograph was taken during fire prevention week, a time to raise public awareness and encourage residents to "have that chimney fixed." The E. Romero Hose and Fire Company used whatever means it had on hand to spread the word. Upon closer inspection, the fire hoses, an extinguisher, fire axe, ladders, and a boy in the truck are visible. (RH.)

After 1899, the Rough Riders held their reunions in various cities. The town went on without the Rough Riders but enjoyed a Cowboys Reunion beginning in 1920 that continued until the 1960s. This picture is from one of the reunions held between 1927 and 1930. New Mexico governor Richard Dillon is on the left, three unidentified people are in the middle, and Chief, owned by a smiling Leonard Stroud, pay homage to the chief executive. (LB.)

The Duncan Opera House was at the corner of Sixth Street and Douglas Avenue. Many smaller Western towns supported opera companies and had performance halls for them as well. Las Vegas was no exception. In addition to hosting musical performances, the Duncan building had a café, jeweler' shop, and a photographer's store. The site is now a drive-through bank branch. (LP.)

This postcard shows both the Montezuma Hotel in the distance and the hot springs complex in the foreground. Part of a train on the Gallinas Canyon/Montezuma spur is visible in the right foreground. Note the zigzag road in the middle of the picture going up the hill to the hotel. The exact date of the photograph is unknown, but it is probably from the 1920s. (TS.)

A New Mexico Normal University Fourth of July float is pictured here some time in the 1920s. This seems be a considerable load to ask one of these hand-cranked early cars to carry. (AL.)

The truck parked in front of Ilfeld's store on the Plaza was for the firm's pickups and deliveries in the 1920s. It had solid rubber tires, which made for a bumpy ride, but then there was no need to check the air pressure. Note the chain drive for the rear wheel and the sacks that are full of rice. (FB.)

E.V. Long and his sons posed for this studio portrait in about 1910. Long was a prominent judge in the area for many years. (DL.)

The Las Vegas Savings Bank was the only bank in town that did not close between 1923 and 1925. It survived to build a new home at the corner of Douglas Avenue and Seventh Street. The building is made of Missouri sandstone, cut, carved, and polished in St. Louis before being shipped to Las Vegas for assembly. This picture is from about 1920. (DL.)

The Neoclassical Revival–style design of the Las Vegas Savings Bank evokes solidity and stability. Today, the Las Vegas Savings Bank, after being Bank of Las Vegas for many years, is Southwest Capital Bank. (DL.)

Construction work began in 1927 on the Federal Building, which stands today on Douglas Avenue and houses the administrative offices of the Las Vegas City School System. (OLOS.)

This was the Immaculate Conception Church before it moved to its present location at Sixth Street and National Street. It stood in the triangular block formed by University Street, Grand Avenue, and Fifth Street. An aerial view of the structure is on page 105. (OLOS.)

In 1930, the *Optic* printing plant was in the same spot as where the paper's office is located today. In 2013, the paper stopped using its press in town and began printing the paper in Los Alamos. The move was necessary because it would have been uneconomical to repair the venerable machinery. (ST.)

The Castañeda Hotel is designed in the same California Mission style and was built at the same time as the Santa Fe Depot. The railway built both the depot and hotel, which was named after one of Coronado's captains, Pedro de Castañeda de Nagera. This postcard of guests leaving for a tour is from about 1920. (DL.)

All that is known about this troupe of minstrels and their leader is the theme of their performance, which is related to the military in some way. The sign refers to a number or numbers of recruits. Perhaps the camera is a clue and was part of the act in some way. (OLOS.)

Despite its fondest hopes, the nation found itself involved in a European war that was called the "war to end all wars." A military installation established just north of town received the name Camp Luna for the commander of Troop F of the 1st US Volunteer Cavalry, the Rough Riders, in the Spanish-American War. Here, a National Guard unit of soldiers, called "doughboys," from Camp Luna parades some time in the 1920s. (OLOS MT.)

This group of World War I veterans prepares to take part in a Fourth of July parade some time in the 1920s. Perhaps the group is taking part in the same parade that is also on this page. St. Anthony's Sanitarium stands in the background. (FB.)

Everybody loves a parade, and this one on the southwest corner of the Plaza in the 1920s appears to be no exception. The two-story building marked with the Rosenwald name still stands, but the distant structure is gone. Others in the picture have undergone different uses over the years. (City of Las Vegas Museum and Rough Rider Memorial Collection, 2011.2.234.)

This is a photograph of Sixth Street and Douglas Avenue in about 1920. People have parked their cars along Sixth and gathered on Douglas in anticipation of a parade. Judging from the patriotic bunting and American flags, it is an Independence Day parade. The 2006 movie *The Astronaut Farmer* used a section of Sixth Street in the distance to represent a bus stop in Amarillo, Texas. (FL.)

The train has stopped in Las Vegas for a few moments as people scramble to board and find their seats in this photograph taken in the late 19th century. Las Vegas has continued to enjoy passenger rail service even as it has declined nationwide. Amtrak's Southwest Chief between Los Angeles and Chicago continues to stop once a day in each direction. (DL.)

These men and a lamb help transform the Las Vegas Military Band on the cover into the Cowboys Band during the early decades of the 20th century. By 1916, the band had changed its name. This picture is from that year or later. (DL.)

This is the approach to Las Vegas on US Route 85 from the south in about 1925. There is a car on the highway at the left side of the picture. The Santa Fe Railroad roundhouse is on the right side of the picture near the horizon, and farther right is the coal chute that fueled the trains when steam was still used. (FL.)

King Stadium was a Works Progress Administration project, part of the nation's effort to recover from the Great Depression. One hundred sixty-eight workers made 17 rows of seats and installed restrooms, stables, and carved terraces. There was also a polo field, steeplechase course, and paddock. As World War II approached, the Army converted Camp Luna to training soldiers, and only the stadium remained. This picture was taken during a 1936 Pentecost service celebration. (DL.)

Climbing on locomotives was not the only thing workers did in the rail yard in Las Vegas. Construction of a nine-stall roundhouse in 1880 meant that mechanics and right-of-way gangs, as well as the depot and train crews, made Las Vegas home. As rail traffic grew through the years, the original roundhouse was enlarged to 16 stalls by 1899. However, the last steam engine was retired from the Santa Fe Railroad in 1956, and the roundhouses closed. (OLOS MS.)

JonesE.LasVegas
MEADOWS HOTEL, EAST LAS VEGAS, N. M.

In 1925, El Fidel Hotel was the scene of a lethal shooting. Judge David Leahy confronted *Albuquerque Tribune* editor Carl Magee in the lobby. Leahy had been target of Magee's editorials and promised revenge. As Leahy attacked, Magee fired a gun and killed a bystander. The jury said Magee was not guilty due to self-defense. He later moved to Oklahoma City, where businesses were trying to deal with downtown parking problems. He is credited with solving them by inventing the parking meter there. (TS.)

The Meadows Hotel, which honored the English meaning of Las Vegas in its title, is El Fidel Hotel today, located on Grand Avenue near the off-ramp from Interstate 25. It attracts numerous guests who are interested in the Magee-Leahy story. This postcard photograph is probably from the 1940s. (TS.)

120

The Budweiser Beer Clydesdale horses pose on Douglas Avenue, probably in the 1940s. The horses are the brand's living symbol and are featured on its television commercials and in appearances throughout the nation. The stores in the background, once situated are on the north side of Douglas Avenue, have been replaced with a parking lot. The buildings are included in the aerial view on page 105. (LF.)

The Army departed in 1891, leaving Fort Union to the elements, which are not kind to adobe. The mud bricks melted away in summer thunderstorms and winter rain. In the 1920s, efforts were begun by Masons and other local groups to establish the fort as a preserve, a goal accomplished in 1956 when the National Park Service acquired it. The picture shows remains of the post's officers' quarters before stabilization. (DL.)

After the Japanese attack on Pearl Harbor, Camp Luna was once again the scene of military training. For this war, artillery and convoy escort training were conducted at the installation on the north edge of Las Vegas. This picture of cannons being fired was taken some time in the 1940s. (LP.)

The Presbyterian mission, established in 1891, has recently been restored and returned to service by its denomination. This photograph is from the 1940s. (TS.)

During World War II, the building at South Gonzalez and Bridge Streets at the southeast corner of the Plaza was a facility for making parachutes. This 1950s photograph shows a class from New Mexico Highlands University but is indicative of the type of work done in the parachute factory that helped win the war. (City of Las Vegas Museum and Rough Rider Memorial Collection, 2009.27.92.)

This is how someone approaching the Plaza on South Pacific Street in the 1930s and 1940s would have seen the route. Notice the directional sign for US Route 85 painted on the wall ahead on the left. Before interstate highways, travelers had to negotiate cities and towns by following markers such as this US 85 sign. It was easy to miss one and quickly get lost. (PSLV.)

The year was 1948, and Harry Truman was fighting for reelection. He pledged to "beat the Republicans and make 'em like it." To get close to the people, he campaigned from the back of a train passing through Las Vegas. He is seen here with New Mexico senator Joseph M. Montoya. KFUN radio aired the president's address live. (FB.)

This is the circulation desk for Rodgers Library at New Mexico Highlands University in the 1950s. The boxy things in the background are card catalogs, which people regularly used not too long ago to find where books were located in the library. The Rodgers building is still in use and located just south of the Donnelly Library and student union building. (DL.)

John Meem designed Rodgers Hall. It is named in honor of Tom Rodgers, a professor of mathematics and academic dean for New Mexico Normal University. The university dedicated the building in 1937. Today, it is the university's administrative offices. (DL.)

The former Montezuma Hotel served as a Baptist college from 1922 to 1930 and a Jesuit seminary from 1937 to 1972. The *El Paso Times* described the seminary this way: "The school trains young men from Mexico to become secular or parish priests in that country. It was . . . located outside Mexico to protect the clergy against such persecution as they had experienced from the Mexican government in the 1920's." (PSLV.)

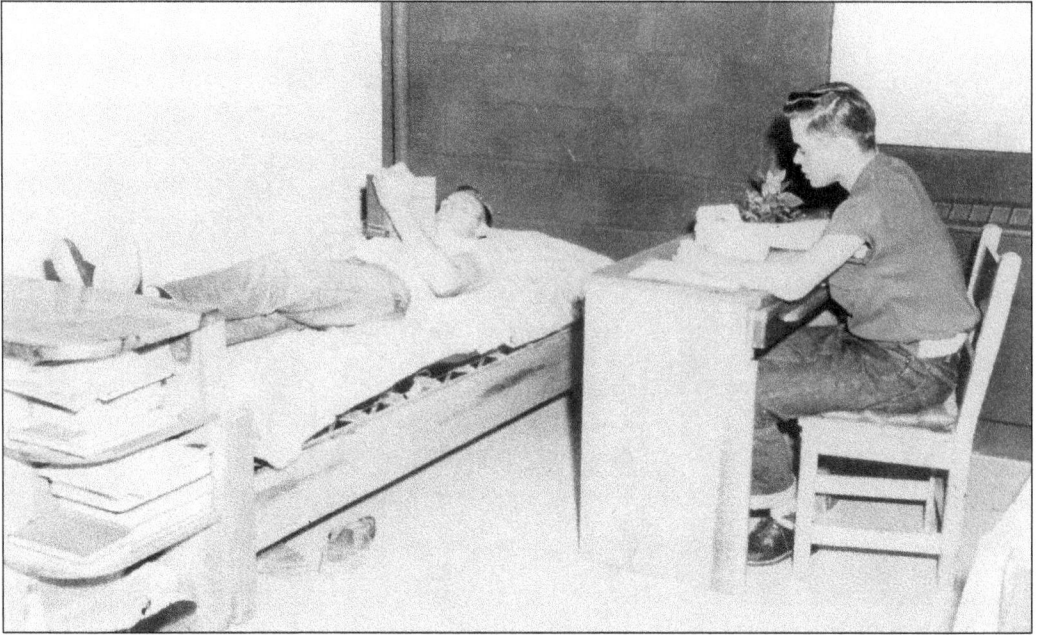

Two New Mexico Highlands University students are in their dorm rooms some time in the 1950s. One works at his desk while the other reads in bed. (DL.)

This church between Las Vegas and Montezuma has an eye-catching exterior that often elicits comments from passing motorists. This picture of the mural is from the 1950s, and the mural itself appears much the same today as it did then. (OLOS.)

BIBLIOGRAPHY

Callon, Milton W. *Las Vegas, New Mexico: The Town That Wouldn't Gamble*. Las Vegas, NM: Las Vegas *Daily Optic*, 1962.

Myrick, David F. *New Mexico's Railroads: A Historical Survey*. Albuquerque: The University of New Mexico Press, 1990.

Perrigo, Lynn. *Gateway to Glorieta: a History of Las Vegas, New Mexico*. Boulder: Pruett Publishing Co., 1982.

Visit us at
arcadiapublishing.com